Building Bridges in Celebrity Studies

Edited by
Jackie Raphael, Basuli Deb and Nidhi Shrivastava

WATERHILL
PUBLISHING

ISBN 978-0-9939938-4-8

The views and opinions expressed herein are those of the authors and do not necessarily reflect the positions of the publisher.

© 2016 Papers are licensed by WaterHill Publishing. Copyrights of individual papers is retained by authors. The papers in this edited volume may not be reproduced in any form or by any means without the prior written permission of the authors.

For the entire volume including cover image and design:
© 2016 WaterHill Publishing, Toronto

Contents

List of Contributors iii

Introduction: Bridging the Gaps Between Celebrity
and Media 1
   Jackie Raphael, Basuli Deb and Nidhi Shrivastava

PART I - Bridging Celebrity Trends and Consumer Perception

Celebrity Influence on Audiences' Consumption Practices as Parents 8
   Elizabeth Fish Hatfield

Front Row Aspirations in the Online Era: Bodies, Accessories and
Fashioning Celebrity 20
   Rebecca Halliday

PART II - Bridging Sensationalised Media and Commodified Celebrities

Selling the Bromance: Sensationalism of the McAvoy/Fassbender
Relationship 32
   Celia Lam and Jackie Raphael

Commodifying Celebrity: Social media, sensationalism, and how the media
plays a role in creating celebrities 45
   Judith Roberts

Quantifying Celebrity: Influence Measurement
in the Digital Age 54
   Andrew Zolides

PART III - Bridging Media Controversy and Celebrity Status

A Persona of Global Controversy: Assange, Snowden, and the Makings of the Digital Information Activist..64
Andrew Munro

Corporate Colonization and the Myth of Authentic Journalism 75
William Huddy

Celebrity Culture and the Canadian Broadcasting Corporation: Jian Ghomeshi, Global Others, and Sexual Violence 84
Kiera Obbard

PART IV - Bridging Women's Issues and Media Representation

The Power of Celebrity Culture and its Response to Rape and Sexual Violence against Women in Post-2012 India.. 96
Nidhi Shrivastava

Media Representations and Angelina Jolie's Elective Mastectomy and Transnational Adoption 107
Basuli Deb

List of Contributors

Basuli Deb, Assistant Professor, UNL, has published a monograph *Transnational Feminist Perspectives on Terror in Literature and Culture* and peer-reviewed articles in, among others, *Frontiers*, *Meridians*, *South Asian Review*, and *Postcolonial Text* where she also guest-edited. Currently she is working on a monograph on celebrity culture, and another on indigeneity/diaspora.

Rebecca Halliday is a PhD Candidate in Communication and Culture at York University in Toronto. She also holds an MA in Theatre and Performance Studies from York. Her work has appeared in *TranscUlturAl: A Journal of Translation and Cultural Studies* and *Fashion Theory: The Journal of Dress, Body & Culture*.

Elizabeth Fish Hatfield serves the Department of Arts and Humanities at University of Houston – Downtown as an Assistant Professor of Interpersonal Communication. Her work focuses on family, gender and culture in the mass media, including issues such as work/life balance, identity, and gender roles.

William Huddy, Ph.D started his broadcast reporting career at KEYT in Santa Barbara (1971), later anchoring newscasts in El Paso, Colorado Springs, Milwaukee, and Fort Myers, Fl. He earned his Ph.D. in Communication Studies (University of Denver, 2012), and teaches at Metropolitan State University, Denver. He can be reached at whuddy@msudenver.edu.

Dr. Celia Lam is a Lecturer in Communications at the University of Notre Dame Australia, Sydney. She is a Centre for Media and Celebrity Studies advisory board member and associate editor of the IAFOR Journal of Media, Communication and Film. Her research focuses on the cultural and aesthetic impact of digital technologies on media production and consumption.

Andrew Munro (PhD) is a Lecturer in Spanish Studies at Griffith University, Australia. His current research focuses on the interrelations of rhetorical genre theory, Peircean semiotics and persona studies.

Kiera Obbard completed her MA in Cultural Studies and Critical Theory at McMaster University, focusing on feminist theory and representations of gender, sexuality and the body in popular culture. Kiera is currently working as an independent scholar and conducts research on gender, violence, and visual culture in a Canadian context.

Dr. Jackie Raphael is a Lecturer in Creative Advertising and Design at Curtin University in Australia. Her research focuses on celebrity, endorsements and bromances. She is an Advisory Board Member of Centre for Media and Celebrity Studies, on the Steering Group of Inter-Disciplinary.Net and *Celebrity Chat* producer. She has published various papers, edited multiple books and organized conferences globally.

Dr. Judith Roberts teaches journalism and communication courses at Louisiana Tech University. She received her Ph.D. in mass communication with a minor in instructional technology from the University of Southern Mississippi. Her research focuses on social media and politics. She also blogs for a fitness website and writes for a north Louisiana magazine.

Nidhi Shrivastava is a PhD candidate at University of Western Ontario. She holds a double masters in South Asian and Women Studies. A regular contributor to *Anokhi Media* and editorial board member of CMCS, she teaches in alternate high school and at University of Connecticut, Storrs.

Andrew Zolides is a PhD Candidate at the University of Wisconsin-Madison. He researches the *influence economy*, an economic framework for understanding strategies celebrities and brands utilize through social media to generate audiences with significant value. Comparing these practices reveals how influence is generated and given value in contemporary neoliberal culture.

Introduction: Bridging the Gaps Between Celebrity and Media

Jackie Raphael, Basuli Deb and Nidhi Shrivastava

Celebrity and Media

Celebrity culture is highly reliant on media representation. Without media attention celebrities are limited in the way they can depict their identities to consumers. While fans can watch their films or listen to their music, they are more informed about their individual personas through the interviews and other media interactions. As technology has progressed many fans are learning about celebrities through their social media accounts. Whether or not this is an authentic representation is unknown, however it is the way the celebrity or their representatives wish to convey their persona. Perceived authenticity is crucial in reflecting the image of a celebrity. While a celebrity has more control over how they are represented today, there is also an increased chance of being criticised on a global scale through social media. This book aims to bridge the gaps between celebrity culture and media involvement. Through four parts and ten chapters, various themes are investigated including trend setting, consumer consumption, impact of social media, sensationalism in reporting, celebrities as a commodity, media scandal creating fame, and feminism.

Many of the themes mentioned have been covered before by biographies and social critiques of celebrities — the former allied to media sketches/academic literature and the later to academic literature.[1] Films studies scholars of the 1970s such as Richard Dyer whose book *Stars* was instrumental in the development of image theory, Laura Mulvey in her article "Visual Pleasure and Narrative Cinema" (1975), and Richard Shickel in biographical *His Pictures in the Papers: A Speculation on Celebrity in America Based on the Life of Douglas Fairbanks, Sr.* (1974) pioneered celebrity research. As the field became interdisciplinary sociological and semiotic inquiries merged with psychological and media studies perspectives. The 80s and 90s saw the publication of Leo Braudy's *The Frenzy of Renown: Fame and Its History* (1986), Richard deCordova's *Picture Personalities: The Emergence of the Star System in America* (1990), and P. David Marshall's *Celebrity and Power: Fame in Contemporary Culture* as the critical lens

---

[1] See Kristin Harmon.

shifted to the sociopolitical concept of celebrity fame. Meanwhile, sociological and cultural studies approaches to celebrity biographies like Shickel's continued. Among them are Leonard J. Leff's *Hemingway and His Conspirators: Hollywood, Scribners, and the Making of American Celebrity Culture* (1997), Georges-Claude Guilbert's *Madonna as Postmodern Myth: How One Star's Self-Construction Rewrites Sex, Gender, Hollywood and the American Dream* (2002), and others. These authors situate celebrities in the larger mechanisms of celebrity production as Jason Toynbee in *Making Popular Music: Musicians, Creativity and Institutions* (2000) and Graeme Turner et al. in *Fame Games: The Production of Celebrity in Australia* (2000). Finally, media studies enters celebrity studies in a vigorously new way through the lens of fandom and gossip in celebrity studies from the 90s as in Camille Bacon-Smith's *Enterprising Women: Television Fandom and the Creation of Popular Myth* (1992) and Jackie Stacey's *Star Gazing: Hollywood Cinema and Female Spectatorship* (1994). Racial and gender identity become other important sites for media analysis of celebrity culture as focus on media representation of celebrities gain critical power through works such as Jeanine Basinger's *A Woman's View: How Hollywood Spoke to Women, 1930–1960* (1993), Martha Gever's *Entertaining Lesbians: Celebrity, Sexuality, and Self-Invention* (2003), and Diane Negra's *Off-White Hollywood: American Culture and Ethnic Female Stardom* (2001).

However, what this book provides is a variety of perspectives on celebrities situated within a transnational domain from the virtual to the material dominated by media/social media culture — whether in the form of celebrity in the age of a global consumerist culture or whistleblowing in global political scandals. It examines fraught intersections of media and social media productions of celebrities, issues of sensationalism, self-productions through controversy, as well as the politics of media ethics and gendered expectations. A collection bridging gaps between media and celebrity thus, is not a production that uncritically understands the relationship between the two as interdependent and symbiotic. Rather one that examines new intellectual and creative energies generated to push the boundaries of our knowledge in celebrity and media studies when we examine the tensions between the two. The goal of such critical rigor is to push these fields along ethical directions that will engage in the constructive work of social justice where media and celebrities combine for an ethical commitment to social transformation. Both media and celebrity culture are crucial parts of people's daily lives, thus a greater understanding of how the two co-exist is essential.

Bridging Ideas

Part I of this book is titled *Bridging Celebrity Trends and Consumer Perception*. Included in this section is a chapter by Elizabeth Hatfield titled *Celebrity Influence on Audiences' Consumption Practices as Parents,* and a chapter by Rebecca Halliday titled *Front Row Aspirations in the Online Era: Bodies, Accessories and Fashioning Celebrity*. These chapters explore how celebrities set trends and what impact they can have on different industries. From fashion fads to parenting prestige, these chapters offer a variety of views on how the conventional as well as new media play a vital role for generating and sustaining such impacts.

While Hatfield explored the trends of celebrity parents impacting on consumers, Halliday examined the importance of a celebrity appearance at fashion shows. Ultimately, celebrities help to set trends and can influence purchasing decisions. However, their authenticity is also significant, as Hatfield discussed. While Hatfeld's chapter investigates printed magazines, Halliday discussed the impacts of social media trends, in particular, the rise of fashion bloggers. Both chapters focused on the power of celebrities and the influence they have on consumers, creating an interesting dialogue for Part I and establishing the significance of celebrity personas.

Following this, Part II is titled *Bridging Sensationalised Media and Commodified Celebrities*. This section focuses on how the media uses these celebrity identities to sell. The first chapter by Celia Lam and Jackie Raphael is titled *Selling the Bromance: Sensationalism of the McAvoy/Fassbender Relationship*, and explores the way the media romanticizes the bromance between Michael Fassbender and James McAvoy to sell the *X-Men* franchise and gain readers. It is established in this chapter that sensationalism is a large part of popular culture reporting. This theme of sensationalism is continued in the next chapter, *Commodifying Celebrity: Social media, sensationalism, and how the media plays a role in creating celebrities* by Judith Roberts, who looks at the ways in which social media has transformed the methods celebrities and politicians use to market their image and persona in the public. As a result, sensationalized reporting has led to them quickly becoming headliners in the news. Her chapter looks at the history of sensationalism focusing on recent and past cases in the news and finally arguing for new ways of implementing media literacy to create active citizens so that they are aware of new and traditional media.

Like Lam and Raphael discussed, celebrities become commodities, used to sell. Andrew Zolides looks at this theme in his chapter titled *Quantifying Celebrity: Influence Measurement in the Digital Age*. He particularly focuses on how current social media produces micro-celebrities (Internet-based), celebrities, and the way brands influence the economy. He argues that services like Q-scores and Klouts are part of what he terms "influence economy", which can be translated into a fiscal economy and is open to any individual with a social media account. From these chapters, it is clear that celebrities are used as commodities to promote and sell a wide range of products and services. Sensationalizing their brand identities and the news surrounding them can help in this promotion.

Part III, titled *Bridging Media Controversy and Celebrity Status,* takes the focus away from Hollywood celebrities and looks at those who become famous due to their media controversy. These chapters also explore the role the media plays in creating these celebrities. The first chapter is by Andrew Munro who looks at *A Persona of Global Controversy: Assange, Snowden, and the Makings of the Digital Information Activist*. It is a study in the contrastive performances with and depiction by the media of celebrity whistleblowers Julian Assange of Wikileaks fame and US National Security Agency contractor Edward Snowden. The chapter examines these performances and media reception as key contributions to the field of persona studies of digital information activists. On the other hand, William Huddy's chapter looks at *Corporate Colonization and the Myth of Authentic Journalism.* It analyzes how the controversy around NBC's Brian Williams transformed his celebrity identity as the ethos of this free thinking seasoned journalist clashed with the notion of 'authentic' reporting under media corporations. The final chapter of this section was written by Kiera Obbard and is titled *Celebrity Culture and the Canadian Broadcasting Corporation: Jian Ghomeshi, Global Others, and Sexual Violence*. Obbard's chapter explores how, in the context of Jian Ghomeshi's sexual abuse scandal, the Canadian Broadcasting Corporation engaged in a project of nation building, demarcating the sexually deviant as the others of the pristine Canadian nationalist imaginary that in turn enabled Canada to remain complicit in a culture of violence against women. The chapters in Part III come together through a thematic focus on media politics around the notion of the ethical.

Part IV of this book also looks at the role that journalists play in reflecting scandalous issues. Titled, *Bridging Women's Issues and Media Representation* this section explores feminist issues. Like Obbard, Nidhi Shrivastava examines the issue of sexual violence in her chapter. The role of women is important in this chapter *The Power of Celebrity Culture and its Response to Rape and Sexual Violence against Women in Post-2012 India*. Using a postcolonial feminist lens to examine a host of media interviews as well as media critiques of Bollywood celebrities, she posits that sexism marks the realm of Indian celebrities. Shrivastava deploys the examples of Kalki Koelchin, Deepika Padukone, and Aamir Khan to compare and contrast the problematic and sexist ways in which Koelchin and Padukone are compelled to justify their positions as advocates of women's rights whereas Khan's persona as a public intellectual is more readily accepted. Basuli Deb also explores the way women are represented in the media through her chapter *Media Representations and Angelina Jolie's Elective Mastectomy and Transnational Adoption*. Much like Hatfield's chapter on celebrity parents and how they are perceived, Deb investigates how Jolie is critiqued in remarkably sexist ways as a mother in tabloids. As well, Deb's examination of the misogynistic media responses to Jolie's elective mastectomy is aligned with Shrivastava's critique of sexism in Bollywood. Studying the trends of transnational adoptions from the global South, she looks at the various types of sexist criticism that celebrities like Jolie and Madonna have received for propagating a brand of celebrity colonialism, which further creates a schism between the haves and have-nots across both the domestic and international divisions of labor. Bringing together Bollywood and Hollywood around critiques of gendered expectations from women celebrities, Part IV offers a transnational feminist archive of sexism that marks the media and celebrity lives in the global south, as well as the global north.

To conclude, this volume traces the current trends that are developing in the entertainment and celebrity industry. The role of media in our times has been complemented by diverse forms of new media, generating conduits for celebrity impacts on the local and the global in ways unforeseen in the past. As the combined forces of the media and social media have brought celebrity social activists into close proximity like never before, such power has disseminated news about social justice work, creating new kinds of celebrities, among them politically dissident hackers. This collection aims not only to bridge gaps between celebrity studies and media studies, but also to examine how bridges between traditional media studies and new media studies can generate innovative synergies in celebrity studies.

Acknowledgements

The editors wish to thank the Centre for Media and Celebrity Studies (CMCS) and the Centre for Ecological, Social, and Informatics Cognitive Research (ESI.CORE) who sponsored the conference *Bridging Gaps: Where is the Persona in Celebrity and Journalism?*, which inspired this book.

References

Bacon-Smith, C. (1992). *Enterprising women: Television fandom and the creation of popular myth*. Philadelphia: University of Pennsylvania Press.

Basinger, J. (1993). *A woman's view: How Hollywood spoke to women, 1930–1960*.

New York: Alfred Knopf.

Braudy, L. (1986). *The frenzy of renown: Fame and its history*. New York: Oxford University Press.

deCordova, R. (1990). *Picture personalities: The emergence of the star system in America*. Urbana & Chicago: University of Illinois Press.

Dyer, R. (1979). *Stars*. London: British Film Institute.

Gever, M. (2003). *Entertaining lesbians: Celebrity, sexuality, and self-invention*. New York: Routledge.

Guilbert, G. (2002). *Madonna as postmodern myth: How one star's self-construction rewrites sex, gender, Hollywood and the American Dream*. Jefferson, NC: McFarland & Co..

Harmon, K. (2005, Spring). Celebrity culture: Bibliographic review. *The HedgeHog Review*, Retreived December 29, 2015.

Jeff, L.L. (1999). *Hemingway and his conspirators: Hollywood, scribners, and the making of American celebrity culture*. Lanham, MD: Rowman & Littlefield.

Marshall, P. D. (1997). *Celebrity and power: Fame in contemporary culture*. Minnesota: University of Minnesota Press.

Mulvey, L. "(1975, Autumn). Visual Pleasure and Narrative Cinema. *Screen*, 6-18.

Negra, D. (2001). *Off-white Hollywood: American culture and ethnic female stardom*. New York: Routledge.

Shickel, R. (1974). *His pictures in the papers: A speculation on celebrity in America based on the life of Douglas Fairbanks, Sr*. New York: Charterhouse.

Stacey, J. (1994). *Star gazing: Hollywood cinema and female spectatorship*. New York: Routledge.

Toynbee, J. (2000). *Making popular music: Musicians, creativity and institutions*. London: Bloomsbury.

Turner, G., Bonner F., & Marshall, P. D. (2000). *Fame games: The production of celebrity in Australia*. Melbourne: Cambridge University Press.

PART I

Bridging Celebrity Trends and Consumer Perception

Celebrity Influence on Audiences' Consumption Practices as Parents

Elizabeth Fish Hatfield

Abstract. This chapter considers how celebrity mothers influence audience members' consumption patterns as mediated role models of good parenting practices. The desire to be seen as 'good mothers' motivates audience members to watch and learn from celebrities parenting in the public eye, whose behaviors are framed positively and negatively by celebrity news outlets. Celebrities become parenting trendsetters for audience members, demonstrating successful parenting through engagement, fashion, and buying the best for their baby. Consumption becomes closely tied with images of good motherhood, for both baby goods and maternity needs. The choices celebrities make, the good mother they portray, and the balance celebrity mothers appear to achieve all communicate a success achieved by celebrities and available to audiences willing to mirror the behaviors of favorite celebrities.

Keywords: Celebrity, consumption, motherhood, authenticity, social learning

Introduction

In a world of 'mommy wars', celebrity parents often offer a media respite for audiences who actively follow them. Unlike popular media coverage of real moms' battles over how to parent, celebrity news frequently bypasses these storylines for a glossed over package of family bliss or extraordinary drama. Douglas and Michaels (2005) refer to the "standards of perfection" (p. 3) expected of mothers today, challenging media messages that constantly reinforce an ideal for motherhood requiring mothers look amazing, have a demanding career, a perfect house, and well behaved children. These celebrity trendsetters frame identity for women as they transition to motherhood, and are furthered by the existence of celebrity role models selected by the media to represent both good and bad mother identities.

Cultural messages about consumption behaviors offer one way mother's perceptions about being a good mother are shaped and managed. Schwartz (1996) wrote: "Consumer capitalism transformed the family from a unit of production into a unit of consumption" (p. 76). The traditional task of shopping for the household remains a mother's responsibility, and mothers find pleasure in buying things for their children, affirming their identity as a "good mom" (Coffey, Siegel & Livingston, 2006, p. 6). Additionally, mothers are encouraged to buy for themselves during pregnancy and beyond to manage their bodies and appearance (O'Donohoe, 2006).

Mothers receive messages about consumption from a variety of sources during pregnancy, including media depictions of celebrity parents also experiencing new parenthood. These celebrities, elevated by fame and glamour, offer role models for audience members who may learn from them, intentionally or unintentionally. This project considers the role of celebrities in creating a culture that closely connects a good parent identity with consumption practices. Using content analysis and focus group data, this chapter seeks to understand how audiences learn from celebrity trendsetters, what impact celebrities have on consumption patterns and perceptions, and consider greater implications for the future of authenticity in celebrity journalism.

Celebrity Culture, Consumption, and Motherhood

During the late decades of the twentieth century, a shift in media coverage of celebrities trampled the long held boundaries for privacy in celebrities' personal lives, and pushed us into what Cashmore (2006) labeled "celebrity culture" (p. 155). The influence of celebrity culture can be seen in the wide-ranging media outlets now regularly covering celebrity stories as news, placing these articles alongside traditional hard news stories for audiences seeking up-to-the-minute information. The celebrity as a newsworthy persona has become mainstream, rather than a topic serving a niche audience of housewives and Hollywood devotees.

The celebrity persona evolves through heavy media coverage, often a combination of planned and unplanned news coverage. The relationship between celebrities and journalists stretches back long into the history of printed media (Marshall, 2006). Marshall argued (2006): "The celebrity embodied that contradiction of being individually elevated and thus relatively unique, but dependent on a new system of 'democratically inspired' value that was derived from popular audiences" (p. 316). Reporting on celebrities during the twentieth century shifted from being a mash-up of second hand stories to being cooperative pieces in which the celebrity supplies the information (Marshall, 2006).

This interest in celebrities' personal lives led to the development of the "celebrity mom profile," (Douglas & Michaels, 2005, p. 16) introduced in women's magazines during the 1960s and 1970s. These stories offered in-depth interviews and photo displays covering celebrity family life for magazines such as *Good Housekeeping* or *Ladies Home Journal*. Central to the celebrity mom profile was the consistent depiction that celebrity motherhood comes easily, is picture perfect, and redefines the celebrity's core identity (Douglas & Michaels, 2005). These profiles are still a common feature in women's magazines and a dominant editorial focus in celebrity gossip magazines. The influence of the celebrity mom profile today extends to actual parenting magazines, whose editorial foci shifted to using celebrities in 2011 as a way to stay more relevant for "hip parents" (Moses, September 19, 2011).

The success and influence of the celebrity mom profile can be understood using a media effects framework. Concepts such as social cognitive theory and social comparison theory position individuals as reliant on others for making sense of one's own experience. With social cognitive theory, celebrities become role models for audiences, offering a mediated understanding of parenthood framed through social rewards and consequences (Bandura, 2002). Social comparison also is at play in celebrity news, as audiences compare themselves to celebrities and make an evaluation of competency as new parents (Alicke, 2000). Both of these concepts take on a greater salience once audiences enter parenthood; stories of celebrity parenting may have more resonance for audiences now experiencing similar life changes (Bandura, 2002). As readers develop parasocial relationships (relationships that feel real even though a reader does not actually know a celebrity) with celebrity role models, they begin to identify with them more strongly, and even modify behavior to satisfy a desire to actually be more like that celebrity (Brown & Frasier, 2004).

The need to feel like a 'good mother' in society may be satisfied by mirroring celebrity role models. Johnston and Swanson (2006) found that mothers actively constructed what constitutes a 'good mother' identity based on a combination of their mothering ideologies and work status. Collett's (2005) participants reported managing their 'good mother' identity through children's appearance and clothing. Indeed, motherhood is one of many identities a woman takes on and can be challenging to integrate into a firmly established personal identity (Bailey, 1999; Haynes, 2005). This is particularly true for type-A women compelled to demand perfection (O'Donohoe, 2006). The celebrity mom profile offers a story of successfully managing work and home life (as all celebrities are ultimately working mothers), often presenting consumption as one replicable way women can act as good mothers.

The centrality of consumption during pregnancy is highlighted by bestselling books such as *Baby Bargains* (Fields & Fields, 2015) and *Best Baby Products* (Gordon, 2009) that navigate the consumption process. Indeed, consuming on behalf of a child is an activity many women welcome during pregnancy. The ultrasound revealing a child's sex signals women to freely engage in consumption of baby goods (Taylor, 2000).

Consumption also characterizes the baby shower, a ritualized stage of pregnancy originally meant to pass knowledge of parenting from generation to generation, but now representing the close relationship of consumption practices and parenthood (Taylor, 2000). Thomsen and Sorenson noted: "Consumption activities have come to replace culturally prescribed rituals, the so-called rites of passage, which support the individual during her transition" (2006, paragraph 6). Their research on stroller advertising emphasized the impact this purchase had on new parents' identity construction as a publicly visible good used in the care of their children. Engaging in consumption practices, such as purchasing items during pregnancy, allows women (and men) to fantasize about their future identities as parents.

Investigating Celebrity Influence on Parent Consumption

To investigate how celebrity role models impact consumption practices of audience members, this project engaged two forms of data as part of a larger study on celebrity parenting. First, a sample of celebrity magazines was analyzed for content using narrative analysis, a qualitative method focused on analyzing stories and their structure (Riessman, 2008). Celebrity magazines offered a contained content form for analyzation, as compared to the Internet and other online venues. Due to the similarity of content between these outlets, and crossover (magazines publishing Instagram photos, for instance), the researcher felt this sample represented the genre overall while offering measurable sampling techniques. A total of 36 issues of *Us Weekly* and *People* magazines were collected for the sample, yielding 160 stories about celebrity parenting as listed in the table of contents. These stories were categorized and evaluated for thematic narratives across the sample.

Additionally, a series of focus groups were held with mothers who follow celebrity media to examine how audiences interpret these stories. The focus groups consisted of two to seven women and allowed for natural conversation about parenting and celebrities similar to unstudied interactions, though the groups followed a semi-structured interview style. The five focus groups contained a total of 22 participants representing the reported audiences for celebrity news publications. Data collected reflected source fluidity for participants who referenced celebrity news gathered from a wide variety of news outlets. Though the total number of participants was moderate, the data indicated that saturation had been met.

After collecting the focus group data, that information was also analyzed using thematic narrative analysis. Similar to traditional thematic analysis, this method allows for emergent themes across the data and seeks to categorize themes as a way of noting trends. The two-part approach to data collection allowed for both a deep knowledge of the actual content of celebrity news, as well as the interpretive understanding expressed by actual audience members. The results of the analysis presented in this chapter consider one key finding from that study: the effects of celebrity trends and consumption perceptions on audience members' experiences as parents. Therefore, this chapter discusses three themes that emerged from the data: creating the celebrity parent persona, consumption as part of a 'good mother' identity, and authenticity in the coverage of celebrity parents.

Discussion

This chapter analyzes the role of the celebrity persona as an influence on parenting and consumption behaviors using the research collected. The central finding illustrates how the celebrity persona develops through positive news coverage, becomes an avenue for connecting consumption practices with the ideal of good parenting, and impacts how audiences evaluate authenticity in an age of inundating media. Please note that participants' names have been changed to allow for anonymity.

Creating the Celebrity Parent Persona

Central to the ability to promote consumption as a good parenting practice is the need to define celebrities as role models. Constructing celebrities as good parents actively involved in their children's lives capitalizes on the audience's great interest in celebrities' private family lives, while simultaneously leveraging the celebrity's existing reputation. Parenting in these magazines becomes inherently gendered, with mothers taking on the primary caregiving role, while fathers periodically step in for "daddy duty" (*Us*, July 23, 2007).

Articles focused on decorating a nursery, communicate the female celebrity's traditional gender role, with images of lavish nurseries carefully designed by the expectant mother. Readers can interpret dad's visual absence in these stories in many ways; a traditional reading might be that dad is 'providing for the family' while mom serves as homemaker (even if she is the better known celebrity). Work for the female celebrity recedes, as her mother identity takes precedence over that of worker. What she is famous for – being an actress, recording artist, philanthropist, etc. – becomes mere context for the story.

Though the nursery serves to reflect the celebrities' glamorous life, key to creating the celebrity mother persona are images that reflect how 'normal' she is. Jaunts to the park and picking up children from school are ways celebrity magazines successfully position celebrities to feel 'just like us.' This duality creates an aspirational reality – grounded in the shared experience of motherhood – that becomes fantasy for readers whose finances and job flexibility may limit their ability to achieve the (work/family) balance celebrities appear to have found. While most audience members understand their lives are quite different from celebrities, parenthood offers a common ground for audience members to connect with celebrities. As focus group participants noted:

> It's something we can relate to. Like, that's not something reserved for celebrities. I can get pregnant just like you can get pregnant. It's just something you have in common. They are going to go through the exact same thing during those nine, ten months. They are going to be looking for the same baby gear. It might, you know obviously they are going to be spending a lot more money and have a lot more support, but sort of, at the most basic level, it's a shared experience. (Audrey)

> It's just one piece of their lives that the rest of us can relate to. Whereas most of their lives we can't relate to, you know because we just don't have houses and servants and drivers and planes and all these things. But we do have kids and if [celebrities] actually are at home, semi-taking care of their own children, then they're being thrown up on, peed on, they're up in the middle of the night, you know. (Destiny)

The commonality of parenthood is a critical part of the role model, creating a comparison for audiences about a relatable topic. The shared experience of parenthood engaged audience members in a more involved way as they paid attention to stories of celebrity parents as a learning tool for cultural norms.

Consumption as Good Motherhood

In addition to creating the celebrity mom persona, celebrity magazines shape the news cycle into a circular process that urges audiences to follow their favorite celebrities like never-ending soap operas. Anything can be news, but changes in celebrity families offer particularly rich content for advertising-driven magazines whose audiences are often moms. Consumption begins during celebrity courtships and weddings, and continues with updates on a celebrity's jeans, designer purses, and award ceremony gowns. The announcement of a celebrity pregnancy and the months to follow further expands coverage of celebrity consumption. For audiences, following celebrity pregnancies begins when the pregnancy is announced, often via these publications. The up-to-the minute news nature of online media pushes this further, allowing news to spread faster.

As a celebrity moves through her pregnancy, typical stories cover updates on the pregnancy, preparation for baby, learning the baby's sex, and the baby shower. Celebrity consumption remains a major part of these stories as parents prepare for their new baby, and becomes an inherent characteristic of the emerging celebrity mother persona. Readers learn of items celebrities buy or receive as gifts for their unborn children – often luxurious goods too expensive for most new moms (Tan, December 24, 2007). As Douglas and Michaels (2005) found, "The celebrity profile insists that truly good, devoted mothering requires lavishing as many material goods on your kids as possible" (p. 132). Readers aspiring to be good mothers can easily find and buy the pictured items in these articles thanks to layouts identifying brands and costs. The presentation of these items sets apart Hollywood babies from the ordinary child – essentially a form of the designer clothes and fabulous houses their parents inhabit.

Consumption within these articles identifies celebrity babies as 'special', but it also signals a stars' ability to be a good parent. The process of consumption visually replaces the baby it honors – a temporary substitute during the nine-month gestation. Showing a celebrity mother with her 'baby booty' demonstrates for readers a socially appropriate, desirable way to prepare for your child. The joy later depicted as a mother looks at her newborn can also be seen as a celebrity takes steps to prepare for the baby. Consuming well translates to parenting well during these early stages in particular. Audience members experiencing pregnancy can consume along with their favorite celebrity.

Not to be overlooked, the celebrity herself transforms during pregnancy, shedding her old persona for the new mother identity. The celebrity impacts audiences by choices for herself, as well as her baby, that influence cultural norms regarding pregnant fashion, bodies, and lifestyles. Participants clearly communicated the social impact of pregnant celebrities:

> I think it's more and more accepted to be pregnant and show you're pregnant in your tight tee shirts instead of a big, old baggy shirt that you used to wear when you're pregnant. And I think [celebrity pregnancies in the media] maybe has something to do with that. (Katie)

> They don't gain as much weight. I was looking at, Rachel Zoe's pregnant now and I'm just like, 'Oh, what is she wearing?' because she's the stylist and all the winter clothes are so ugly. So, I was all excited to like, look and see. You can't even tell she's pregnant half the time. (Courtney)

> I think at the same time we can identify with them, it's also, at the same time it's the opposite, they're stars. What are they going to do, you know

with their nursery, what is their nursery going to look like and you know they are going to have beautiful babies, because they are beautiful people. (Sarah)

Participants' clothing decisions during pregnancy reflected the trends set by pregnant celebrities, with an appreciation that celebrities had made pregnancy itself fashionable. The most powerful example of this would be Duchess Kate Middleton, whose maternity clothing selections almost immediately sold out once the media covered them (Kindelan, March 26, 2015). Notably affordable choices intermingled with high end designers allowed audiences to copy Kate's style, as *Hollywood Life* reporter Britney King (March 20, 2015) reported: "You don't have to be The Duchess of Cambridge to have amazing maternity style!" Audiences are encouraged to watch and learn from celebrities, whose iconic pregnancies become consumption opportunities.

Authenticity in Coverage of Celebrity Parents

With the celebrity mom persona elevated, and her consumption choices idealized, audiences must sort through information seeking authenticity. Though participants identified that many of the images in celebrity magazines are constructed public relations opportunities, what remained authentic for audiences was what could be seen in those pictures. Audiences made sense of photo stories by analyzing the choices a celebrity made for her child(ren) in the picture. Consumption practices, such as buying 'the same baby gear', were evaluated differently for celebrities who have the freedom to buy the best without budgetary limitations. Their choices became elevated, acquiring a status of worth and value for participants above and beyond their function. Even so, participants noted the functional nature of caring for a baby, incorporating normal baby goods with the luxury items. "[Celebrities] are just going to get what their child needs. That is what we do too. Not everything has to be really expensive. They are going to get what they need and what's best for their kid," said focus group participant Claire. Participants reported analyzing photos for familiar products. Seeing baby products being used in photos, especially 'candid' images, communicated authentic choice on the part of the celebrity:

> I use cloth diapers and I found out Alison Sweeney uses the same brand of cloth diapers. I was like, wow. Ok. That's pretty cool. Maybe these are pretty good ones out there. Validation, that's the word. (Kristie)

> [Kourtney Kardashian's son] Mason has a little Sophie the Giraffe and I was like, 'Oh, Caleb has a Sophie the Giraffe!' (Susan)

When a celebrity chose the same baby items, this validated participants' parenting choices, endorsing the product's value whether paid or not.

The gray area of paid promotions was not discussed in these focus groups, though this certainly remains a possibility. Arguably, photos of celebrities acting 'just like us' rather than selfies and Instagram-type shots actually communicated a more authentic use of the product. Learning that a photo served to promote a certain product would have undermined the celebrity's authenticity and the authenticity of her motherhood overall.

Media frames also impacted audiences and their understanding of a product. Stories of bad parenting, while less common, shaped participants' own behaviors. For example, one participant remembered a comparison of good and bad mothering:

> I remember the baby's name. Jessica Alba didn't put the sunshade on top of her little baby in the stroller, BAD MOMMY. You know good mommy had a little baseball cap on her baby so the sun wouldn't get in her eyes. So now I'm constantly like, 'Oh my gosh, am I a good mom or a bad mom?' (Susan)

As no parent wants to have what participants called the "Britney Spears parenting moments," articles like the one referenced above resonate with audiences. Negative publicity translated to learning experiences. Here, audiences interpreted that sun shades and protection are part of good parenting, and readers wanting to be good parents can engage in consumption of sunscreen, hats, and stroller shades to achieve that goal. Ultimately, audiences demonstrated a nuanced reading of stories reflecting their content and level of depth, evaluating some stories as more impactful than others in shaping their understanding of good parenthood.

Conclusion

The celebrity persona emerges as role model for audiences, demonstrating a success at balancing new parenthood with work and life, and celebrity magazines often highlight the many ways audiences can emulate that lifestyle through consumption practices. However, the evolving nature of authenticity creates challenges for both celebrities and the celebrity news media, whose symbiotic relationship requires them both to capture audiences. Authenticity in the current environment becomes challenging to negotiate for audiences seeking that feeling of closeness with their parasocial, celebrity friend. The incredible growth of the celebrity news industry, now a $3 billion dollar enterprise, has changed how celebrities themselves engage audiences, with a significant increase in celebrity social media usage, offering celebrities' greater control of their own image (Rutenberg, May 21, 2011).

As a result, audiences receive information about celebrities from a variety of sources, each authentic and inauthentic in their own ways. For respected publications and websites, authenticity emerges from a presumed journalistic standard, while blogs and social media sites maintain authenticity through the celebrity's own voice. However, the public relations industry now manages much of celebrity social network activity (Clayton, January 22, 2013), emerging as another caveat for audiences sorting through information overload for gossip truth. Regardless of source, audiences remain willing to "suspend disbelief" (Hermes, 1995) as they follow celebrity stories.

In the search for truth, celebrity pregnancy becomes a story one cannot hide. The visible nature of pregnancy authenticates the story, one the celebrity news industry supports as a positive driver for revenue-focused content. As focus group participant Claire said, "Its continual news. You can't always guarantee a scandal, but you can guarantee someone is having a baby." The celebrity mom becomes a visual representation of motherhood for audiences watching their transition to this new role. Fans learn from their experiences through media framing of news stories, including parenthood stories. As celebrities emerge as "good moms" (usually) within media stories, these media frames negotiate with lived experiences to shape readers' understandings of their own experience as mothers. The demonstration of consumption as an easy way for parents to feel good about oneself builds on the existing cultural codes that connect consumption with beauty and femininity. Mothers are simply shown one additional way consumption can shape their identity. For journalists, the responsibility to create a cultural understanding of parenthood demands more than a two-dimensional portrait, an idealized image of celebrity home life. The power of the celebrity persona shapes how parents today understand the experience of parenthood, and the 24-hour news cycle only pushes this phenomenon further. The future of this impact must be considered cautiously. In the meantime, the guilty pleasure of engaging celebrity media for moms continues.

Acknowledgments

With sincere gratitude, I would like to acknowledge the time and effort of my advisor, Dr. Srividya Ramasubramanian, whose guidance during the completion of this research was invaluable. I will always be grateful for your mentoring and friendship.

References

Alicke, M. D. (2000). Evaluating social comparison targets. In J. Suls & L. Wheeler (Eds.), *Handbook of social comparison: Theory and research* (p. 271-294). New York: Kluwer Academic/Plenum Publishers.

Bandura, A. (2002). Social cognitive theory. In J. Bryant & D. Zillman (Eds.) *Media effects: Advances in theory and research, 2nd edition* (p. 121-153). Mahwah, New Jersey: Lawrence Erlbaum.

Bailey, L. (1999). Refracted selves? A study of changes in self-identity in the transition to motherhood. *Sociology, 33*(2), 335-352.

Brown, W. J., & Fraser, B. P. (2004). Celebrity identification in entertainment-education. In A. Singhal, M. Cody, E. Rogers, & M. Sabido (Eds.) *Entertainment-education and social change: History, research, and practice* (p. 97-116). Mahwah, NJ: Lawrence Erlbaum Associates.

Cashmore, E. (2006). *Celebrity/culture.* New York: Routledge.

Clayton, T. (January 22, 2013). 5 ways celebrities' social media presence evolved in 2012. Retrieved from: http://www.huffingtonpost.com/thomas-clayton/celebrities-social-media_b_2529151.html.

Coffey, T., Siegel, D., & Livingston, G. (2006). *Marketing to the new superconsumer: Mom and kid.* Ithaca, NY: Paramount Market Publishers.

Douglas, S., & Michaels, M. (2005). *The mommy myth: The idealization of motherhood and how it has undermined women.* New York: Free Press.

Fields, D., & Fields, A. (2015). *Baby bargains, 11th edition.* Boulder, CO: Windsor Peak Press.

Fox, G. (1999). Families in the media: Reflections on the public scrutiny of private behavior. *Journal of Marriage and the Family, 61* (4), 821-830.

Gordon, S. (2009). *Best baby products (Consumer reports best baby products).* Yonkers, NY: Consumer Reports.

Haynes, K. (2004). Transforming identities: Accounting professionals and the transition to motherhood. Working paper. Department of Management Studies, University of York, York.

Hermes, J. (1995). *Reading women's magazines: An analysis of everyday media use.* Cambridge, MA: Polity Press.

Johnston, D., & Swanson, D. (2006). Constructing the "good mother": The experience of mothering ideologies by work status. *Sex Roles, 54*, 509-519.

Kindelan, K. (March 26, 2015). 5 takeaways from Duchess Kate's maternity style. ABC News. Retrieved 10/1/2015 from: http://abcnews.go.com/Entertainment/takeaways-duchess-kates-maternity-style/story?id=29925591

Marshall, P. D. (2006). Intimately intertwined in the most public way: Celebrity and journalism. In P.D. Marshall (Ed.) *The celebrity culture reader* (p. 315-323). New York: Routledge.

Moses, L. (September 19, 2011). 'Parenting' going the celebrity route. Retrieved from AdWeek. Retrieved 9/24/2015 from: http://www.adweek.com/news/press/parenting-going-celebrity-route-134918

O'Donohoe, S. (2006). Yummy mummies: The clamor of glamour in advertising to mothers. *Advertising & Society Review, 7*(3). Retrieved 9/24/2015 from http://muse.jhu.edu.lib-ezproxy.tamu.edu:2048/journals/advertising_and_society_review/v007/7.3odonohoe.html

Riessman, C. (2008). *Narrative methods for the human sciences.* Thousand Oaks, CA: Sage Publications.

Rutenberg, J. (May 21, 2011). The gossip machine: Churning out cash. Retrieved 9/24/2015 from: http://www.nytimes.com/2011/05/22/us/22gossip.html?pagewanted=1&partner=rss&emc=rss&_r=0

Schwartz, D. (1996). Women as mothers. In P.M. Lester (Ed.) *Images that injure: Pictorial stereotypes in the media* (p. 75-80). Westport, CT: Praeger Paperback.

Taylor, J. S. (2000). Of sonograms and baby prams: Prenatal diagnosis, pregnancy and consumption. *Feminist Studies, 26*(2), 391-418.

Thomsen, T., & Sorensen, E. (2006). The first four-wheeled status symbol: Pram consumption as a vehicle for the construction of motherhood identity. *Journal of Marketing Management, 22*(9), 907-927.

Front Row Aspirations in the Online Era: Bodies, Accessories and Fashioning Celebrity

Rebecca Halliday

Abstract. This chapter uses the fashion show as a site to examine fashion's instantiation and contestation of new forms of celebrity, as well as celebrities' increased visibility in the front rows, in the online era. The fashion show's current incarnation, transmitted and proliferated online, qualifies as a *media ritual* (Couldry, 2012): a cultural event that reinforces media institutions' dominance. The presence of celebrities increases coverage and enhances fashion houses' cultural status. Online media has facilitated the infiltration of certain characters into high fashion, and the fashion show itself, disrupting industrial hierarchies. High fashion has consecrated media personalities, actresses and directors as It Girls and 'fashion celebrities,' known for their fashion connections and appearances at fashion shows (Church Gibson, 2012). In 2009, high fashion designers invited fashion bloggers to fashion shows, causing uproar among members of the traditional press. Both fashion celebrities and fashion bloggers possess specific personas, in the service of fashion, cultivated via textual narration and photographs (Sill, 2008; Titton, 2015). Roach (2007) outlines that an ethereal 'It-Effect' is created through a societal fetishization of bodies and accessories. Drawing from Roach, this chapter contends that high fashion positions fashion celebrities and fashion bloggers as aspirational figures but requires that these individuals conform to a specific aesthetic ideal. Using actress Sienna Miller and blogger Tavi Gevinson as examples, this chapter draws parallels between academic and press discussions of fashion celebrities and of fashion bloggers, locating references to hair, skin, teeth and accessories as focal points of scrutiny and emblems of acceptance.

Keywords: fashion, celebrity, persona, blogger, aspirational

Introduction

The contemporary fashion show is a one-off live performance of brief duration during which a fashion house presents its upcoming seasonal collection to industrial insiders. The audience is comprised of retail buyers, media personnel and a roster of invited clientele that includes elite customers, It-personalities specific to fashion or to the local cultural scene, and celebrities. In the past decade, online media have fundamentally altered the structures, formats, processes and timeframes of fashion communication and commerce. The fashion show has transformed into an *online* spectacle, live streamed in 'real time' and archived for consumers' later access. Photographs of the indoor, outdoor and backstage arenas proliferate on press websites, blogs and social media platforms. This instant and international circulation offers unprecedented public exposure to individuals associated with high fashion. Further, online media has facilitated the infiltration of certain media celebrities and non-celebrities into the exclusive realm of high fashion, disrupting fashion's entrenched industrial hierarchies. This chapter parallels academic and press discussions of media celebrities, film actresses and It Girls accepted into high fashion, and the press's reaction to the rise of another fashion persona, the blogger. Fashion bloggers, individuals with a recreational or professional interest in fashion but without pre-existing, traditional press credentials, have attained a notable amount of cultural influence. This chapter contends that high fashion, via the fashion show, positions celebrities and fashion bloggers as aspirational figures whose presence lends status to fashion houses and brands, and who embody consumer culture narratives of identity and class performance. These individuals' presence reflects high fashion's attempt to pre-select and to retain certain embodied ideals that confirm its cultural and class dominance. Examples of film actresses and bloggers demonstrate that industrial tensions around the admittance of new fashion insiders center on bodies and accessories.

Fashion and/as Embodied Class

This chapter incorporates a broad characterization of high fashion that includes both couture and ready-to-wear fashion, and that refers both to a specific editorial aesthetic and to a price echelon. This conceptualization of fashion is predicated on Pierre Bourdieu's (1984) statement that fashion communicates social distinction. Based on his empirical observations of socioeconomic classes in France in the 1960s, Bourdieu declared that consumer choices in cultural and aesthetic products both reflect and reinforce social hierarchies (1984, p. 7). High-end fashions and luxury brand markers function as "emblems" of class status (Bourdieu, 1984, p. 249). Fashion scholars have referenced Bourdieu's (1993) concept of the 'field of cultural production' to describe fashion's industrial structures and members' accumulation, investment and display of economic and cultural capital. Bourdieu's field is a dynamic structure comprised of individuals that occupy positions of influence, and formed from the social relations between them. Entwistle and Rocamora (2006) documented the social interactions of London Fashion Week and described Fashion Week, and each fashion show, as a literal, structured manifestation of the field. Like the field, the fashion show venue has boundaries: admittance means that one holds a position within the field, and barriers and gates delineate membership to the literal inclusion of some and the exclusion of others (Entwistle & Rocamora, 2006, p. 738). The rows, or risers, of seats position attendees according to influence. Those members that possess the most capital, "the more powerful bodies," are seated in the front rows, and become a visual focal point for other members

(Entwistle & Rocamora, 2006, p. 744). Entwistle and Rocamora identified a type of capital "specific to the field of fashion," and termed this 'fashion capital' (2006, p. 740). Fashion capital is embodied and indeed performed via social practices, the wearing of fashionable clothes and the maintenance of one's physical appearance (Entwistle & Rocamora, 2006, pp. 744-748). Couldry (2012) posited a form of 'media-related capital': a charismatic persona and a savviness in the use of media possessed by persons such as newscasters, hosts, celebrities, athletes and politicians (p. 140). The celebrities that attend fashion shows possess both fashion capital and media-related capital. Furthermore, one's presence at a fashion show signifies class status. The fashion show audience member is essential to the production of desire not just because of the fashion capital that he or she embodies but also because of the dominant class status that he or she represents. Each audience member possesses, or appears to possess, sufficient economic capital to purchase garments from the collection, or at similar price points. The consumer audience, viewing online fashion show content, assumes that celebrities in particular can afford the clothes.

Celebrities at the Mediated Fashion Show

The fashion show's current incarnation assumes the criteria for Couldry's (2012) definition of a 'media ritual.' Media rituals are mediated cultural events with a broad reach that incite and focus intense public sentiment and thereby reassert media institutions' political and market clout (Couldry, 2012, p. 66). Examples include talk shows; reality television shows; political events or incidents; sporting events and athletic competitions; awards ceremonies; and the deaths of prominent celebrities. Fashion show footage has been mediated in different forms since the earliest decades of cinema (Evans, 2001). However, until the last decade, footage was screened or broadcast after the event had ended. Fashion companies have come to use numerous media platforms and tools to focus consumer attention on the online fashion show as a specific cultural event, and to foster social affiliations around brands. Companies highlight the presence of celebrities to entice consumers to tune in to live streams and to contribute to social media conversations; in fact, celebrities, as representatives of the upper class, are often paid to attend (Sherman, 2010).

The presence of celebrities at fashion shows can be traced to couture fashion's cross-promotions and cross-pollinations with theatre in the modern period (Evans, 2001, 2013; Kaplan & Stowell, 1994; Schweitzer, 2009; Troy, 2004). In the early 1900s, as mass production and consumption muddied social hierarchies, actresses became instruments for a reaffirmation of class in consumer culture. Schweitzer (2009) documented that American "actresses, as celebrities," attained a "status as a trendsetter and role model" (p. 8). Actresses sported the latest designer fashions in theatre productions and in "photographs and illustrations" in "class-oriented" fashion magazines (Schweitzer, 2009, p. 8). The rise of cinema enhanced actresses' influence and reach as ambassadors of social ideals and aspirational consumption (Berry, 2000; Church Gibson, 2012). One of the earliest references to actresses attending fashion shows (then called 'mannequin parades') is contained in the memoirs of the couturière Lucile (Lady Duff Gordon). Her first mannequin parade, in 1911, was attended by "famous actresses, more famous courtesans, women of title, women of fashion, with a good sprinkling of equally famous men, artists, men of letters and diplomats" (1932, p. 187, as cited in Evans, 2001, p. 305). The press's focus on celebrities at fashion shows reached a fever pitch towards the turn of the millennium, though this emphasis served different functions depending on national and commercial markets. Buckley and Gundle (2000) declared that couture fashion houses use celebrities to build an aura of glamour around the event, and by extension the fashion house:

> The 'fashion weeks' of London, Paris, Milan and New York give rise to ample coverage of runway shows by leading designers which are conceived precisely to capture press and media attention. The concentration of designer brands, fabulous frocks, name models and celebrity guests, all under the glare of publicity and fêted with lavish hospitality, amounts to an irresistible cocktail of all that is desirable in contemporary commercial couture. (p. 38)

While most consumers cannot afford couture, consumers' fascination with the fashion house translates to purchases of its cosmetics, perfumes, accessories and other franchised products (see also Taylor, 2000, p. 130). Discussing *The Guardian*'s coverage of fashion shows, Rocamora (2001) stated that the embodied presence of the recognizable celebrity creates interest. Celebrities "are famous bodies that add glamorous prestige to the dress they look at or wear" (Rocamora, 2001, p. 130). *The Guardian* prioritizes discussion of celebrity attendees over descriptions of the clothes (Rocamora, 2001, p. 130). However, even as mentions of celebrities create interest in fashion collections, *The Guardian* also names celebrities to "reposition high fashion ... within the field of popular culture" (Rocamora, 2001, pp. 131-132). Celebrities are rendered relatable, but the paradoxical effect is to enhance consumers' aspirations to emulate their social enactments. Summarizing Richard Dyer's (1979/2004) theorization of the 'star system,' Warner (2014) drew a distinction between a star's lifestyle and the "*display* of lifestyle," the latter of which attracts public or consumer interest and forms the star's persona (p. 111, emphasis in original). To illuminate the display of lifestyle as insubstantial or superficial threatens to destabilize fashion's foundations in class hierarchies (Warner, 2014, p. 111). However, fashion helps the star to form an aspirational persona that entices consumers to imagine their own "reinvention and transformation" (Warner, 2014, p. 111). Notions of class still underlie consumers' social and aesthetic ambitions and determine what fashions the consumer can afford to wear (Warner, 2014, p. 111). Attendance at fashion shows positions celebrities as aspirational personas: both members of the field of fashion through their professional associations with brands and members of an elite class with purchasing power.

Celebrities' appearances at fashion shows are documented in the traditional press and via online and social media, both during live-stream broadcasts and in photographs. Fashion line Topshop Unique broadcasts "pre-shows," in which a host announces the celebrities that will attend, and interviews celebrities (including bloggers) as they arrive. Photographs of celebrities are frequently the most circulated of fashion show photographs on Twitter. Mentions of front row celebrities in tweets rank higher in word counts than references to clothes and collections.

[1] Front row celebrities often wear clothes from the brand presenting the collection (in some instances, the same pieces as the models). For example, celebrities attending Topshop Unique's Autumn/Winter 2015 fashion show wore pieces from the previous season's collection that were about to arrive in stores.

Formation of Fashion Personas

In the online era, Church Gibson (2012) has observed unprecedented interconnections between fashion and celebrity. She identified new types of 'fashion celebrities,' recognizable due to their involvement in the field of fashion. Her list included media personalities Olivia Palermo and Alexa Chung, British actresses Sienna Miller and Emma Watson, American actresses Chloë Sevigny and Kirsten Dunst, and American director Sophia Coppola. Other examples include actresses Kate Bosworth and Diane Kruger. These women are just as famous, if not more so, for their fashion credibility as for their film resumes. Fashion celebrities "champion the fashionable ideal": they maintain a slim physique; wear cutting-edge clothes; collaborate with brands on collections; pose for magazines and advertising campaigns; endorse skincare products; and appear at parties and fashion shows (Church

---

[1] This observation comes from word cloud text analysis of 1,000 tweets pertaining to the Burberry Prorsum Spring/Summer 2016 fashion show and 1,000 tweets pertaining to the Topshop Unique Spring/Summer 2016 fashion show, at London Fashion Week. Results were obtained using Netlytic social media analytic software.

Gibson, 2012, p. 23). Crucially, Church Gibson emphasized that these celebrities align themselves with *high* fashion, as opposed to a more mainstream, sexualized form of glamour (2012, p. 23). Like the fashion blogger, these celebrities have been "welcomed into the coveted front-row seats at the seasonal couture shows, replacing the leading fashion journalists who traditionally occupied those seats" and causing resentment among the press at or near the top of fashion's hierarchies (Church Gibson, 2012, p. 23).

Both fashion celebrities and fashion bloggers use a combination of clothes, textual content and photographs to construct a persona connected to fashion and media. Warner (2014) observed that television actresses with ties to high fashion function as 'cultural intermediaries' (Bourdieu, 1984). Such individuals mediate between cultural producers and consumers, and "educate audiences" in specific designers and fashion trends (Warner, 2014, pp. 18-19). Notions of class are integral to the semiotics of these "star personae" and their associated roles (Warner, 2014, p. 19). Fashion celebrities, visible in fashion show front rows and on social media, fulfill this same mediating function. Sill (2008) outlined the role of the fashion portrait, a photographic genre, in the creation of an actress's star persona. This persona must fit with the public's existing perceptions of the actress and her sartorial preferences, or her familiar 'look' (Sill, 2008, p. 135). Fashion bloggers can also be considered cultural intermediaries; indeed, Pedroni (2015) identified the practice as a 'subfield' of fashion. Rocamora (2011) observed that the combination of fashion, narration, photographs and media facilitates experimentation in "identity construction" and feminine representation (p. 410). Titton (2015) theorized bloggers' formation of an authoritative 'fashionable persona': a process that "unfolds in a *narrative practice* – in the form of the production of fashion texts ... and in *bodily practices* – in the form of the enactment and incorporation of a certain 'grammar' of corporeal postures and behaviour" (p. 209, emphasis in original). Findlay (2015) demonstrated that personal fashion blogs, those that document an author's outfits and fashion philosophies, have become increasingly aspirational as the medium has earned high fashion's notice, and as authors have become fashion arbiters. Bloggers' appearances have become homogenized into an aesthetic that is "uniformly youthful, slender, attractive, and dress[ed] almost exclusively in 'designer' labels" (Findlay, 2015, p. 173). The formation and function of both fashion celebrity and fashion blogger personas center on the construction and positioning of bodies: on appearance, enactment, comportment and dress. This positioning, in social life and in the fashion show space, encapsulates field and class structures.

Roach (2007) defined the 'It-Effect' as an element of charisma or allure, often possessed by celebrities or public figures. The 'It-Effect,' or 'It,' results from a confluence of public fascination and embodiment. For Roach, the phenomenon of 'It,' like that of glamour, is ethereal and difficult to pin down, but the characteristic is recognizable, and often revered, in those special individuals that possess It. Though this quality is innate, the 'It-Effect' can, like the persona, be cultivated and mediated. Roach stated that It does not equate to attractiveness, but 'It' nonetheless creates "mass attraction" (2007, p. 3). The 'It-Effect' is manifested through a societal fetishization of body parts, such as hair, skin, teeth and bone, and of accessories, such as hats, that act as talismans for our cultural obsession with certain individuals. Such fixation, however, takes both positive and destructive forms: the 'It-Effect' creates fandom, adoration, desire or reverence, but 'It' can also provoke scrutiny, envy, hatred or violence (Roach, 2007, p. 17). Central to the operation of the 'It-Effect' is a need for 'synthetic experience,' the "vicarious" identification with and embodiment of another person's life (Roach, 2007, p. 28). While high fashion positions certain celebrities as 'It Girls,' the fashion show features its attendees as elites for consumers' vicarious identification.

Bodies and Accessories in High Fashion

Church Gibson (2012) described several instances in which actresses or media personalities that seek entrance into high fashion, as a field or as a social realm, are scrutinized for, or forced to alter, aspects of their appearance. While high fashion has historically promoted rigid physical and aesthetic ideals, in these scenarios, the focal points for criticism are those same features that are conduits for the It-Effect. Church Gibson cited a scene from the 2009 documentary feature *The September Issue*, which details the production of *US Vogue*'s annual Fall fashion issue, in 2007, under infamous editor Anna Wintour:

> The cover girl for this issue and for the central shoot … is the celebrity Sienna Miller, taken to Rome to be photographed by Mario Testino. She has a hard time. Her hair is deemed unsatisfactory and so a wig is specially made but then discarded because it's 'not working out'. Finally, the offending hair, described on screen as 'lank and lifeless,' is tied up in a knot on top of her head. Even then, the cover image, when presented, is met with criticism: 'Look at her teeth,' murmurs Wintour. (2012, p. 134)

The cover photograph is Photoshopped (Odell, 2009, cited in Church Gibson, 2012, p. 79). Wintour's concerns with Miller's appearance focus on two channels for the It-Effect, hair and teeth. While Miller has been a fashion It Girl in the mainstream press due to her bohemian personal 'look', her high fashion initiation, in the form of her appearance on the cover of *Vogue*'s iconic annual issue, requires adherence to higher editorial dictates. In recent seasons, Miller has embodied this ideal. In February 2015, she sat front row at the Calvin Klein show at Autumn/Winter New York Fashion Week, next to Wintour, with a side-parted, asymmetrical bob and white overcoat with oversized lapels. *The Daily Mail* reported that Wintour was "blindsided" by Miller's fashionable appearance (Dodge, 2015, para. 2). Church Gibson remarked that high fashion prefers paler skin (2012, p. 31). Miller's skin appears notably more tanned in the documentary, and in photographs from its premiere in 2009, than it appears in 2015.

In 2009, prominent fashion designers sent fashion show invitations to fashion bloggers for the first time: this symbolic industrial recognition took the form of literal access to the event (Findlay, 2015). More notably, companies whisked them to front row seats to the consternation of accredited fashion editors that had worked for decades to even get close. Several of the earliest successful personal fashion bloggers built their personas around a specific feature or accessory: *Style Bubble*'s Susanna Lau has thick bangs; *Bryanboy*'s Bryan Grey Yambao wears distinctive sunglasses; and the title of Jane Aldridge's *Sea of Shoes* speaks for itself. But it was blogger Tavi Gevinson who bore the brunt of the media attention, and "intense criticism," because, at the time of her entrance onto the fashion show circuit in 2009, on the heels of notice for her blog *Style Rookie*, she was 12 years old (Rocamora, 2012, p. 100). Journalists devoted several columns to whether Gevinson was equipped to write about fashion. One tweet, however, encapsulated both the press's wariness of her field ascendance, and their frustration with bloggers' presence in the front row. At the January 25, 2010 couture show for Christian Dior (then under head designer John Galliano), an editor for Italian fashion magazine *Grazia* was seated behind Gevinson, wearing an enormous bow by the milliner Stephen Jones. The editor tweeted a photograph of the second-row perspective behind the headpiece, with the caption, "At Dior. Not best pleased to be watching couture through 13 year old Tavi's hat" (Sauers, 2010). Gevinson's hat became a beacon for industry furor over fashion's hierarchical upset, enacted in the fashion show risers. Veteran critic Sarah Mower (2010) commented on Gevinson's hair at the same presentation:

> At the Dior show, trying to fight my way backstage to get a quote from John Galliano, I nearly fell over a tiny, grey-haired woman who, from the back, I took to be a septuagenarian Japanese fashion fanatic, as she was dressed head-to-toe in Comme des Garçons. When she was ushered into the inner sanctum before me, and turned around, I saw, with a sick lurch, that it was Tavi Gevinson, the 14-year-old fashion blogger from Chicago [who had] recently dyed her hair the trendiest colour. (para. 8)

Mower at first described Gevinson as a high fashion eccentric, which indicated partial acceptance, or as a novelty act that high fashion might entertain, if just for a limited time. Subsequently, however, Mower mocked

Gevinson for subscribing to current trends as if she was merely a non-self-aware teenager. A later comment that perhaps Gevinson should be in school echoed this tone (Mower, 2010, para. 9). Tellingly, Mower expressed horror as Galliano permitted Gevinson to interview him before members of the press.[2] In a 2012 interview, Gevinson poked fun at herself for her ensemble at Christian Dior, but also admonished high fashion's standards:

> I was at the absolute height of my awkward phase when I went to Fashion Week. It's supposed to be this place with the most beautiful people in the world, and I was this incredibly tiny, gray-haired – what's the word? – gnome. ... I think it's hilarious that in the middle of these rooms full of tall, skinny people in black was this tiny weird person. (Oatman-Stanford, 2012, para. 11)

Gevinson declared that the press turned "a giant bow into a metaphor for the death of fashion journalism," highlighting the fact that critics focused their professional resentment onto her features and accessories (Oatman-Stanford, 2012, para. 12). Gevinson has since become a media mogul. She is founder and editor-in-chief of *Rookie Magazine* and has acted in film and on Broadway. While she has broadened her sphere beyond high fashion, she nonetheless remains consecrated as a fashion insider. She appeared on the cover of *NYLON*'s October 2014 annual It Girl Issue, her hair cut in a side-parted, asymmetrical bob notably similar to Sienna Miller's. In July 2015, she became an ambassador for Clinique skincare, in a brand campaign targeted to millennial consumers (Wischhover, 2015).

Conclusion

This chapter has demonstrated parallels in the formation of the persona of celebrities and bloggers associated with the elite social and industrial realm of high fashion. Both sets of individuals are held up as aspirational figures that can incite vicarious identification and build consumer desire and brand affiliations. Furthermore, press and academic discourses on the entrance of celebrities and bloggers into high fashion bear distinct similarities, as individuals are scrutinized for specific physical features and accessories that must conform to a set of embodied aesthetic ideals. These same features and accessories, in a broader sense, function as focal points, or mediums, for public fascination with certain celebrities. The traditional press's reaction to these individuals' presence in prominent positions at fashion shows reflects

---

[2] While both the *Grazia* editor and Mower remark on Gevinson's age, she would have been 13 on January 25, 2010. This discrepancy suggests that columnists did not care about listing an accurate number so much as stressing her youth as a marker of inexperience.

high fashion's need to preserve its class dominance. The fashion show operates as the literal site of contestations between the fashion press and newcomers to the field. It is crucial to continue to examine how online media alters fashion's hierarchies and redefines the types and roles of the celebrities present at these mediated events, as well as how companies use and position celebrities and fashion bloggers to enhance brand profiles and fuel consumer aspiration.

References

Berry, S. (2000). *Screen style: Fashion and femininity in 1930s Hollywood.* Minneapolis: University of Minnesota Press.

Bourdieu, P. (1984). *Distinction: A social critique of the judgment of taste.* (R. Nice, Trans.). Cambridge, UK: Harvard University Press.

Bourdieu, P. (1993). *The field of cultural production: Essays on art and literature.* Ed. R. Johnson. New York: Columbia University Press.

Buckley, R., & Gundle, S. (2000). Fashion and glamour. In I. Griffiths & N. White (Eds.), *The fashion business: Theory, practice, image* (pp. 37-54). Oxford and New York: Berg.

Church Gibson, P. (2012). *Fashion and celebrity culture.* London: Berg.

Couldry, N. (2012). *Media, society, world: Social theory and digital media practice.* Cambridge, MA: Polity Press.

Dodge, S. (2015, Feb. 19). Sienna Miller is a vision in white as she captivates Anna Wintour front row at the Calvin Klein show during NYFW. *Mail Online.* Retrieved from http://www.dailymail.co.uk/tvshowbiz/article-2960672/Sienna-Miller-vision-white-captivates-Anna-Wintour-row-Calvin-Klein-NYFW.html

Dyer, R. (1979/2004). *Stars.* London: BFI Publishing.

Entwistle, J., & Rocamora, A. (2006). The field of fashion materialized: A study of London Fashion Week. *Sociology, 40*(4), 735-751. doi: 10.1177/0038038506065158

Evans, C. (2001). The enchanted spectacle. *Fashion Theory: The Journal of Dress, Body & Culture, 5*(3), 271-310. http://dx.doi.org.ezproxy.library.yorku.ca/10.2752/136270401778960865

Evans, C. (2013). *The mechanical smile: Modernism and the first fashion shows in France and America, 1900-1929.* New Haven, CT: Yale University Press.

Findlay, R. (2015). The short, passionate, and close-knit history of personal style blogs. *Fashion Theory: The Journal of Dress, Body & Culture, 19*(2), 157-178. doi: 10.2752/175174115X14168357992319

Kaplan, J. H., & Stowell, S. (1994). *Theatre and fashion: Oscar Wilde to the Suffragettes.* New York: Cambridge University Press.

Mower, S. (2010, Feb. 3). Pre-fall 2010 heralds the return of classic dressing, brown leather and Tavi Gevinson. *The Telegraph.* Retrieved from http://fashion.telegraph.co.uk/article/TMG7138882/Pre-fall-collections-herald-the-return-of-classics-brown-leather-returns-and-Tavi-Gevinson-Pret-a-rapporter.html

Oatman-Stanford, H. (2012, Nov. 28). Nostalgia is magic: Tavi Gevinson remixes teen culture. *Collectors Weekly.* Retrieved from http://www.collectorsweekly.com/articles/tavi-gevinson-remixes-teen-culture/

Pedroni, M. (2015). 'Stumbling on the heels of my blog': Career, forms of capital, and strategies in the (sub)field of fashion blogging. *Fashion Theory: The Journal of Dress, Body & Culture, 19*(2), 179 - 200. doi: 10.2752/175174115X14168357992355

Roach, J. (2007). *It.* Ann Arbor, MI: University of Michigan Press.

Rocamora, A. (2001). High fashion and pop fashion: The symbolic production of fashion in *Le Monde* and *The Guardian. Fashion Theory: The Journal of Dress, Body & Culture, 5*(2), 123-142. doi: 10.2752/136270401779108626

Rocamora, A. (2011). Personal fashion blogs: Screens and mirrors in digital self-portraits. *Fashion Theory: The Journal of Dress, Body & Culture, 15*(4), 407-424. doi: 10.2752/175174111X13115179149794

Rocamora, A. (2012). Hypertextuality and remediation in the fashion media. *Journalism Practice, 6*(1), 92-106. doi: 10.1080/17512786.2011.622914

Sauers, J. (2010, Jan. 25). Tempest in a trilby: Fashion blogger Tavi Gevinson's hated hat. *Jezebel.* Retrieved from http://jezebel.com/5456560/tempest-in-a-trilby-fashion-blogger-tavi-gevinsons-hated-hat

Schweitzer, M. (2009). *When Broadway was the runway: Theater, fashion, and American culture.* Philadelphia: University of Pennsylvania Press.

Sherman, L. (2010, Feb. 3). How much brands pay for celebs to sit in their front rows. *Fashionista.* Retrieved from http://fashionista.com/2010/02/how-much-fashion-brands-pay-for-celebrities-to-sit-in-their-front-rows.

Sill, B. (2008). Stardom and fashion: On the representation of female movie stars and their fashion(able) image in magazines and advertising campaigns. In E. Shinkle (Ed.), *Fashion as photograph: Viewing and reviewing images of fashion* (pp. 127-140). London and New York: I.B. Tauris.

Taylor, L. (2000). The Hilfiger factor and the flexible commercial world of couture. In I. Griffiths & N. White (Eds.), *The fashion business: Theory, practice, image* (pp. 121-142). Oxford and New York: Berg.

Titton, M. (2015). Fashionable personae: Self-identity and enactments of fashion narratives in fashion blogs. *Fashion Theory: The Journal of Dress, Body & Culture, 19*(2), 201-220. doi: 10.2752.175174115X14168357992391

Troy, N. J. (2004). *Couture culture: A study in modern art and fashion.* Cambridge, MA: MIT Press.

Warner, H. (2014). *Fashion on television: Identity and celebrity culture.* London and New York: Bloomsbury Academic.

Wischhover, C. (2015). Tavi Gevinson, new face of Clinique, talks anti-aging and looking like an alien. *Fashionista.* Retrieved from http://fashionista.com/2015/07/tavi-gevinson-clinique-interview.

PART II

Bridging Sensationalised Media and Commodified Celebrities

Selling the Bromance: Sensationalism of the McAvoy/Fassbender Relationship

Celia Lam and Jackie Raphael

Abstract. Celebrity culture is celebrated in the media daily. The Web 2.0 paradigm shift has resulted in a convergent media environment that has affected both celebrity culture and the practice of journalism. When breaking through media clutter is paramount to both increased visibility and readership, capturing public imagination has become key to success. This has precipitated a mutually reliant relationship between celebrities wishing to promote themselves and their work, and entertainment journalists seeking to fulfill their mandate and grow followers. As a result, the media is sensationalizing details and the celebrities are being used as a commodity to sell stories and films. With an increased curiosity in bromances, celebrities are now using their bonds and banter to promote their movies and gain online hits. A prime example of this is the bromance between X-Men actors, Michael Fassbender and James McAvoy. This chapter identifies how their bromance is shaped by media, analyzing the role journalists play in promoting and branding. Through content and semiotic analysis of three articles the intricate performative and representational relationship between reporter and celebrity is explored. As a result it is made evident that journalists can transform the context of an interview through their own observations, using specific terms – in this case romanticized words – to sensationalize an article. This in turn can impact on how audiences view a celebrity's identity and can help promote their image and film.

Keywords: celebrity bromance, romanticizing, X-Men, sensationalism

Introduction

The celebrity is an amalgamated entity, formed in the primary text (Fiske, 1987) of initial circulation, and subsequently embellished in texts of secondary circulation (O'Shaugnessy & Stadler, 2012). P David Marshall (2010) sees in this mediated construction of identity, a representational culture, in which "a production of the self [is] specifically dependent upon a very elaborate and powerful media culture" (p. 38). Thus, while celebrity figures, specifically actors, come to prominence in the on-screen context of performance, it is in the arena of wider media coverage that their persona is consolidated and perpetuated.

As a prominent part of media culture, the celebrity profile piece is often charged with claims of blatant fawning and pandering to public relations demands. However, they offer practical insights into the construction of a persona conceived at the intersection of journalism, public relations and celebrity culture. Here the celebrity figure is literally written into being, where highly personalized encounters making claims of exclusivity simultaneously contribute to the creation of a unified image. As such they are often used as a dual marking device to promote individuals and attract readership in a media saturated environment.

Similarly, close celebrity friendships are evoked in popular press to generate excitement and stimulate gossip. An iteration of such friendships is the 'bromance', defined by Michael DeAngelis (2014) as an "emotionally intense bond between presumably straight males who demonstrate an openness to intimacy that they neither regard, acknowledge, avow, nor express sexually" (p.1). Bromances offer a view of male intimacy that toys with tropes of homosexuality however, resists 'natural' inclinations towards romantic conclusions. As a marketing device, the application of the term to a close celebrity friendship captures audience interest and stimulates fan creations, thereby ensuring some degree of longevity in an increasingly forgetful popular consciousness. The role of celebrity profiles, and the journalists who compose them, on the creation and sensationalism of celebrity bromances will be explored in this chapter. Content and semiotic analysis was conducted on three profile pieces to examine the role of both journalist and celebrity in the construction of the bromance between actors Michael Fassbender and James McAvoy in the wake of the films *X-Men First Class* (2011) and *X-Men Days of Future Past* (2014).

Profiling Fassbender and McAvoy

The profile piece renders celebrity figures as characters, presented through various 'scenes' in which the profiler recounts their engagement to construct an image (generally favorable, often predetermined) of the celebrity in his/her habitat. Thus setting, language and imagery is key to the generation of symbolism that aids the projection of a specific celebrity persona, and will be examined in each of the three profile pieces selected for analysis.

Published within a ten-month period (November 2013 – September 2014), the profiles were produced against the backdrop of the film *X-Men: Days of Future Past*. Writing early in 2013, reporter Zach Baron visited Montreal during production of the film to speak with Michael Fassbender for *GQ*. Almost a year later during the promotional run for the release of the film, both Fassbender and James McAvoy are interviewed by Alex Bhattacharji for *Details*, while later that year McAvoy is profiled in *Out* by Paul Flynn.

The release of the profiles coincides with the production and release cycle of *X-Men: Days of Future Past*. As such they are useful mediums through which to analyze the role of print media in film promotion. Additionally, they are works in which both 'partners' of the bromance are represented individually and together (both McAvoy and Fassbender are mentioned in the other's profile). Thus, the profile is revealing of the representational processes of individual celebrity figures, and also of the impact that casual presentation has on the construction of a unified celebrity persona. While all three magazines publish print and online editions, the online versions of the profiles are the focus of analysis in this chapter.

Methodology and Results

Content analysis was conducted on the three profile pieces with a specific focus on terminology used to characterize the actors as individuals, and as a pair. Words and phrases that highlighted personality traits were identified and categorized into themes. Direct quotes were attributed to either actor, while other text was attributed to the journalist.

Analysis was completed independently by both authors and verified, with discussion over themes on which there was disparity. Both authors conducted an initial reading of all three profiles to identify broad themes emergent in the texts. Four themes were identified after the initial reading: 'Professional', 'Hyper masculine', and 'Performed'. 'Bromance' was identified as a theme with three categories, 'Frat boy', 'Brotherly' and 'Romanticized'. Upon completion of the analysis, further themes emerged: 'Affable', 'Family orientated', 'Grounded' and 'Normal'. The amount of times either actor swore was also recorded, as were references to films and *X-Men* in particular.

GQ Profile

The *GQ* profile contained a total of 104 characterizing words or phrases. The three most common characterizations of Michael Fassbender are 'Hyper-masculine', with 24 phrases, followed by 'Frat boy' (23) and 'Professional' (22). James McAvoy is characterized as 'Affable', 'Hyper-masculine' (3), and 'Normal' (2). The actors are represented together as 'Hyper-masculine' (2) and sharing a 'Bromance': 2 instances categorized as 'Frat boy' and 1 'Brotherly'. A total of 10 phrases alluded to characters portrayed by the actors in films, with 4 specifically referencing the *X-Men* films. Full results are listed in Table 1.

Table 1. Characterizing terminology in *GQ* profile featuring Michael Fassbender.

Theme	MF[1]	JM	Theme	Combined
Affable	4	3	Bromance: Brotherly	1
Family orientated	0	0	Bromance: Fratboy	2
Frat boy	23	0	Hyper-masculine	2
Grounded	2	0		
Hyper-masculine	24	3		
Normal	0	2		
Professional	22	0		
Swearing	2	0		
Other Reference				
General	10			
X-Men	4		**Total terms**	104

Out Profile

The *Out* profile contained a total of 67 characterizing words or phrases. The three most common characterizations of McAvoy are 'Professional' (21), 'Family orientated' (7), 'Grounded'/'Normal' (5). 11 instances of swearing are recorded, the majority (10) presented as quotes from McAvoy. Together, the actors are mostly characterized as 'Performed' (4). 5 phrases alluded to characters portrayed by McAvoy in films, with 2 specifically referencing the *X-Men* films. Full results are listed in Table 2.

Table 2. Characterizing terminology in *Out* profile featuring James McAvoy.

Theme	JM	Theme	Combined
Affable	3	Bromance: Brotherly	1
Family orientated	7	Performed	4
Frat boy	2		
Grounded	5		
Hyper-masculine	1		
Normal	5		
Professional	21		
Swearing	11		
Other Reference			
General	5		
X-Men	2	**Total terms**	67

---

[1] In all tables, Michael Fassbender is represented by the initials MF, and James McAvoy by JM.

Details Profile

The *Details* profile contained a total of 176 characterizing words or phrases. Fassbender is characterized as 'Professional', 'Hyper-masculine' and 'Normal' (7) most frequently. McAvoy is most often characterized as 'Family orientated' (9), 'Hyper-masculine' and 'Normal' (4). In total McAvoy swore more than Fassbender, with a record of 16 instances to Fassbender's 1. Their 'Bromance' is most often categorized as 'Romanticized' (19), and based on 'Banter' (18). They were also considered 'Hyper-masculine' (9), creating a 'Frat boy' (7) bond, and 'Professional' (6). *X-Men* films were referenced 25 times, while other performances were referenced 18 times. Full results are presented in Table 3.

Table 3. Characterizing terminology in *Details* profile.

Theme	MF	JM	Theme	Combined
Affable	2	0	Bromance: Banter and Finishing off sentences	18
Family orientated	1	9	Bromance: Brotherly	13
Frat boy	1	1	Bromance: Frat boy	7
Grounded	0	0	Bromance: Romanticised	19
Hyper-masculine	7	4	Hyper-masculine	9
Normal	7	4	Performed	0
Professional	7	1	Professional	6
Swearing	1	16		
Other Reference				
General	18			
X-Men	25		**Total terms**	176

Analysis

Individual Profiles: The GQ Cover Story: Michael Fassbender (GQ) and James F*****G McAvoy (Out)

The magazines featuring the individual profiles on the actors cater to two distinctly different target audiences. *GQ* is an international magazine featuring cars, fashion, and lifestyle, targeted at a male audience. *Out* is a LGBT magazine featuring fashion, culture, the arts, and political issues pertinent to the LGBT community.

In November 2013, Michael Fassbender was featured in a *GQ* cover story. The feature photo accompanying the profile presents Fassbender in mud-splattered clothing atop a motorbike. He is cropped center frame in a pose that commands attention. An expanse of wilderness behind him suggests a daredevil attitude, while the setting of the interview at a racetrack conforms to an image of stereotypical masculinity.

McAvoy appears on the cover of the September edition for *Out* in 2014. The cover image is a headshot of McAvoy, who looks directly at the camera with his body positioned evenly. He is dressed simply, against a non-descript white background. The neutrality of the pose and setting is offset by the intensity of McAvoy's expression; a gaze bordering on anger. It is an image that contradicts the jovial persona found in other media accounts. However, it is supported by the title, *James F*****G McAvoy*, a reference to the actor's penchant for the expletive. Thus, the photo and title form the impression of a complicated figure whose external façade masks a closely guarded interior.

As mentioned, the *GQ* profile predominantly depicts Fassbender as a hyper-masculine individual with the rebelliousness of a frat boy, while also a hard working professional. The profile is presented as an account of reporter Zach Baron's afternoon with Fassbender. Baron (2013) adopts a first person prose like tone, occasionally employing descriptors such as "rakish" to describe Fassbender. However, for the most part he shapes his characterization through descriptive passages of their interactions and conversation, allowing the anecdotes to illustrate his persona. While Fassbender's identity is primarily constructed through Baron's words (Figure 1), quotes are used to reinforce the suggested image. As evidence of his frat boy nature, Baron (2013) simply offers Fassbender's words: "'I need to fart'".

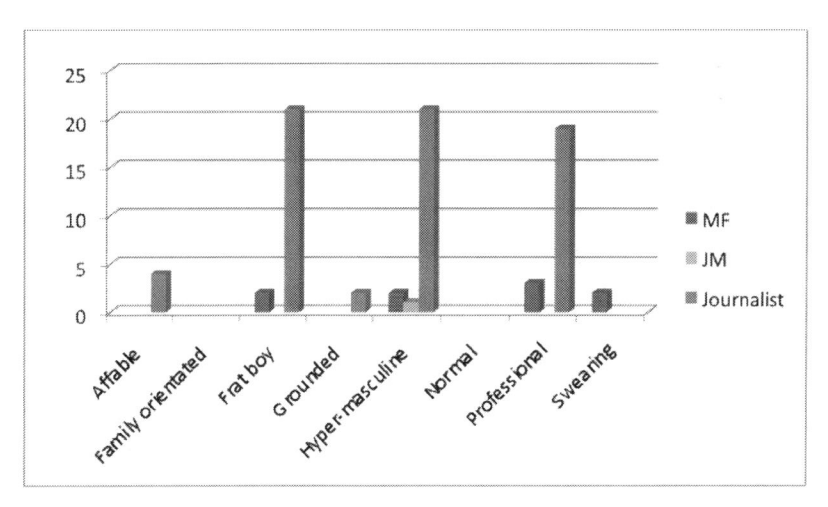

Fig.1. Characterization of Michael Fassbender in *GQ*

Baron mainly characterizes McAvoy as affable, hyper-masculine, and normal (Table 1). However, through contrasts with Fassbender's rebellious attitude towards rules (McAvoy chides Fassbender for overtaking on the racetrack), Baron subtly suggests McAvoy as the most responsible of their pair.

Unlike Baron, who shares the page with Fassbender in *GQ*, Paul Flynn is almost absent in his *Out* profile on McAvoy. For the most part he quotes McAvoy, allowing his verbal expression to flavor the persona. Through a series of anecdotes Flynn constructs a professional figure that is extremely talented yet normal, grounded it is suggested, due to his family orientated nature. However, the maturity of the professional is tempered by his constant swearing (10 instances in total) and frat boy mischievousness, two traits Flynn presents almost entirely through McAvoy's own words (Figure 2).

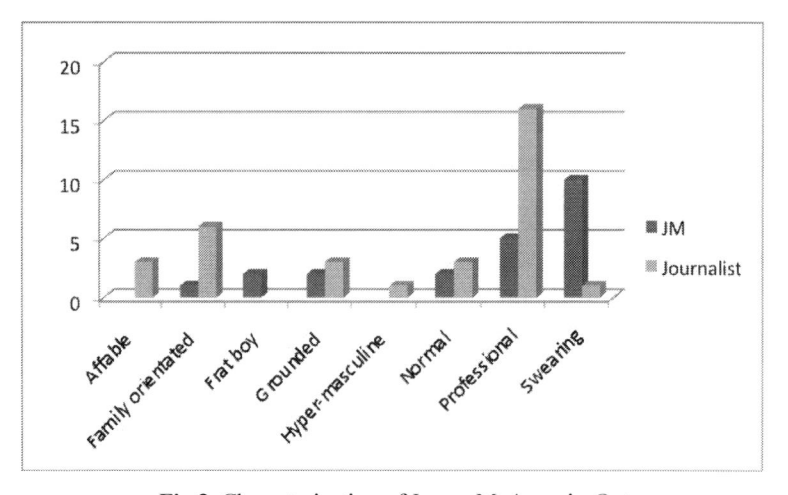

Fig.2. Characterization of James McAvoy in *Out*

Combined representation of the actors is markedly different between the two profiles, although neither mentions the term bromance. In *GQ*, Baron (2013) characterizes them as close friends with strong masculine overtones. He uses phrases such as "fraternal hug" to acknowledge their intimacy but codes it in a 'brotherly' context (Table 3). In the *Out* profile the relationship is accounted for in pragmatic, if not slightly cynical terms. Flynn (2014) characterizes the pair as an "affable Celtic double act" presented for junket interviewers. The revelation of a strategic approach to the display of their friendship undermines some of the genuineness of their closeness by constructing it as a performance (Table 2). However, this differs greatly to the *Details* profile, where the reporter purposefully adds evidence of their 'authentic' relationship.

Combined Profile: "Super Friends: Michael Fassbender and James McAvoy" (Details)

Details is a men's lifestyle magazine covering advice on fashion, health and grooming, as well as articles on culture and trends. In the June/July issue, Fassbender was chosen for the cover, while the profile was based on an interview with both Fassbender and McAvoy. The headline and lead of the *Details* profile by Alex Bhattacharji sets the tone of the article, which focuses on the bromance of Fassbender and McAvoy. The headline refers to the men as "Super Friends", using a pun to play off their superhero characters (Bhattacharji, 2014). Leading into the interview Bhattacharji (2014) states that they met up at a pub to talk about "the meaning of true bromance". The setting is repeated throughout the article to reinforce their hyper-masculine and friendly personas. Throughout the article Bhattacharji (2014) transcribes their conversation and romanticizes their friendship through his own observations, using phrases such as:

- "kindred spirits"
- "onscreen reunion"
- "the connection crystallized"
- "pat his friend on the back"
- "good mate"
- "close friend and co-star"

The series of photographs chosen to accompany this profile were also intentional.

The individual photographs were specifically paired together to denote particular meanings. The first series of paired images shows Fassbender and McAvoy as cool and sexy. These connotations derive from their relaxed body language, intense facial expressions and fashionable attire. The second set of photographs are displayed so that Fassbender is facing McAvoy and the image is taken from a lower angle portraying Fassbender as masculine and powerful. The third set of photos seems to draw focus to their crotches. This is particularly true for McAvoy, based on the angle of the photograph. He is shown glaring into the distance with his fist tightly closed. This conveys the notion of strength. It also places focus on his wedding ring, adding to his family-orientated persona. The seemingly deliberate focus of these images signifies a sexual undertone. The final picture in the profile shows both men hugging. They appear comfortable and relaxed in this close proximity, reinforcing their bond. Ultimately, all the images in this profile have been carefully selected and composed to help depict the bromance between the actors.

The transcripts are more authentic in reflecting the closeness of the actors, conveying the way they finish off each other's sentences and create banter. For example Bhattacharji (2014) transcribed[1]:

> JM: The only time I am dishonest ... when I make shit up or when I deflect ... is when I'm being asked something that is –
> MF: About somebody you don't like?
> JM: Totally. Then I'm a lying bastard. I'm like, 'Michael, he's one of the finest.'
> MF: He's like, 'He's such a good guy.'

This banter is consistent across all their interviews together, which reinforces their bromantic image.

Bhattacharji (2014) continues the movie related puns with the subheading "First-Class Friends", while also taking another opportunity to mention their bond. Bhattacharji's (2014) first sentence in this section reads; "If life were as poetic as they would like it to be, McAvoy and Fassbender would have bonded while making *Band of Brothers* back in 2000." The journalist is adding a romanticized analysis of their friendship, suggesting it is tragic that they did not become friends sooner. Bhattacharji (2014) continues with "their bromance blossomed a decade later". Not only has the journalist directly used the term bromance again in the profile, but has also used the word "blossomed", to add romantic emphasis.

As demonstrated in Figure 3, the majority of romanticized bromantic moments in this article came from the journalist, however the actors did provide some of their own statements that conveyed their closeness. McAvoy stated:

> Before Michael and I even met, I was already willing to go with him and be open to him, because I was like, 'This guy's fuckin' brilliant' ... Not to be too fuckin' up your ass or anything like that, but the thing that elevated *First Class* for me was working with you (Bhattacharji, 2014).

With comments like this, McAvoy is contributing to the bromance intrigue. Fassbender stated; "I had had admiration from a distance" (Bhattacharji, 2014). Thus, suggesting their friendship also included fandom.

---

[1] Bhattacharji transcribed the interview using the actor's initials to indicate who was speaking. JM represents James McAvoy, while MF stands for Michael Fassbender.

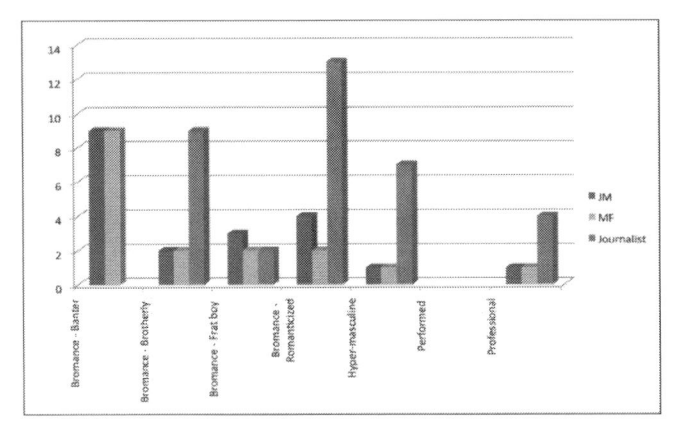

Fig. 3. Characterization of Bromance in *Details* profile.

Throughout the interview McAvoy and Fassbender provide the stories they know the media and fans want to hear. They mention stories relating to BB guns and a golf buggy, which convey their fun personas. These stories also add authenticity to their friendship by providing evidence of their hanging out on set. However, the regular mentioning of these stories in interviews, may also be perceived as less genuine and a part of their duo performance, as suggested in the *Out* profile. Yet, it is clear that the *Details* profile does not share this perspective.

Bhattacharji (2014) again added his analysis of their bond stating:

> As deep and abiding as it is, the friendship is defined by the differences in their lives in a way familiar to many men in their thirties. One is settled down, with a wife and a child, ensconced in a quiet neighbourhood … The other is still in the messy bachelor pad he's had for years.

Drawing this comparison, Bhattacharji relates their friendship back to other men of their age and established Fassbender as a hyper-masculine bachelor while McAvoy is the family orientated man who swears a lot (shown in Table 3). This suggests why people care so much about their bromance, because it is relatable. They either have friends like them or want to be their friend. This was established in fan comments analyzed in previous research (Raphael & Lam, 2015).

In mentioning their busy lives Bhattacharji (2014) explained; "they text, send each other videos, and are thick as thieves when working, as they were while filming". The reporter seems to find it important to reinforce the authenticity of their bromance by mentioning the contact they have outside of filming together and suggesting that time together is not considered work. "'It's not a contrivance at all. I love the guy,' McAvoy says, turning to Fassbender, 'I do mourn your absence sometimes when I'm working with lesser dudes'" (Bhattacharji, 2014). McAvoy is again enhancing the shared bromance identity.

Bhattacharji (2014) concludes the profile by describing that McAvoy and Fassbender were planning "their next adventure: a track day, to race motorcycles". The actors are likely to have chosen to mention this in front of the reporter to add credibility to their bromance. The activity described further reinforces their masculine and fun personas, which was also reflected in the *GQ* profile.

The *Details* profile finishes with a transcription of Fassbender and McAvoy talking, after the journalist left to go to the bathroom. They joke about leaving and about smoking making them appear cool (Bhattacharji, 2014). Finishing with this banter, again reinforces their image and the purpose of the profile. While the interview was conducted to promote their film, the actors and the journalist are aware of the intrigue behind their bromance, thus they both draw attention to this through the content of discussion, the banter between the actors and the romanticized observations of the interviewer (Figure 3).

Selling the Bromance

The publics' perception of celebrity personas is based on the way a celebrity dresses, speaks and acts. The celebrity's career decisions, publicity and interviews also impact on their identity. When a celebrity is in a famous relationship, they often become power-couples, such as Brad Pitt and Angelina Jolie. However, even George Clooney marrying Amal Alamuddin, has transformed his brand and made her famous. Similarly, Hollywood friendships are also of media interest and become a commodity when trying to gain consumer attention. Thus, Clooney and Pitt's bromance has been of public interest since they collaborated on *Ocean's Eleven* (2001). The media plays a significant role in constructing celebrity images and drawing focus to particular facets of their lives. It is evident in the profiles explored in this case study that all journalists chose to focus on, or at the very least mention, the Fassbender and McAvoy friendship, even when the other actor was not the subject of the profile.

As shown in the case study, the relationship between the co-stars are expressed in various ways. The *GQ* profile focuses on their masculine frat boy image, the *Out* profile suggests the cynical perspective of a friendship staged for promotional purposes, while the *Details* profile romanticized their friendship and used the term bromance repeatedly. The *GQ* and *Out* articles also used key words such as "buddy" (Baron, 2013) and "double act" (Flynn, 2014) to refer to Fassbender and McAvoy, reinforcing their closeness more subtly. The actors have chosen to utilize their combined identity to their advantage by telling stories of their time spent together and allowing banter to flow between them in interviews. This helps to enhance their fun personas and draw attention to their film. Evidently, bromances can be a strong promotional tool and can highly impact on a brand identity.

Conclusion

Analysis of the profiles reveals nuances in the presentation of the two celebrity figures, as well as an engagement with their pre-existing image of a bromantic pair. Fassbender's portrayal as a rebellious bachelor is fairly consistent. However, a multifaceted representation of McAvoy's persona can be traced through the three profiles. In the *GQ* profile, McAvoy is presented as the most responsible of the pair, partly reinforced in the *Out* profile. However, his interactions with Fassbender in the *Details* profile constructs him as an equal partner, if not leader, of their frat boy behavior.

The *Details* profile also presented the most direct illustration of collaboration between celebrity figure and reporter to perpetuate a pre-existing image. The banter between McAvoy and Fassbender, is reflective of their close friendship, while also reinforcing their wider cultural status as a 'couple'. However, it is the reporter's deliberate use of romanticized terminology, and choice of quotes, that emphasizes this characterization. It is further reinforced in the choice of images accompanying the profile. Their friendship, suggested as close in the *GQ* and *Out* profiles, is sensationalized as a strong ongoing bromance. Thus, while the actors project a certain persona through their enacted bromance it is through the contextualizing voice of the reporter, as both witness to and medium for the performance, that a unified identity emerges.

Ultimately, a celebrity profile is always going to include the point of view of the journalist and have a specific angle that they wish to write from, which can pre-determine the perspective of the article. While it is the ethical responsibility of journalists not to sensationalize, it seems to be a large part of popular culture reporting. Whether a bromance is authentic or not, it is a commodity for studios selling films and journalists selling stories. Thus both celebrity and journalist play a role in commoditizing and perpetuating specific public persona.

References

Baron, Z. (2013, October 14), The GQ Cover Story: Michael Fassbender. *GQ*. Retrieved from, http://www.gq.com/entertainment/celebrities/201311/michael-fassbender-cover-story-november-2013?currentPage=1

Bhattacharji, A. (2014, July 1), Super Friends: Michael Fassbender and James McAvoy. *Details*. Retrieved from http://www.details.com/culture-trends/cover-stars/201406/michael-fassbender-james-mcavoy-interview-x-men-days-of-future-past?currentPage=1

DeAngelis, M. (2014). *Reading the Bromance: Homosocial Relationships in Film and Television*. Detroit: Wayne State University Press.

Fiske, J. (1987). *Television Culture*. London: Methuen.

Flynn, P. (2014, September 15), James F*****G McAvoy. *Out*. Retrieved from http://www.out.com/entertainment/movies/2014/09/15/james-mcavoy-fame-films-f-word

Marshall, P. D. (2010). The promotion and presentation of the self: Celebrity as marker of presentational media. *Celebrity Studies*, *1*(1), 35-48.

O'Shaughnessy, M., & Stadler, J. (2012). *Media and Society*. Victoria: Oxford University Press.

Raphael, J., & Lam, C. (2015, July). *The Cultural Power Behind the X-Men Bromance*. Paper presented at the IAFOR European Conference on Arts & Humanities, Brighton, UK.

Shuler Donner, L. (Producer), & Singer, B. (Director). (2014). *X-Men: Days of Future Past* [Motion picture]. United States: 20th Century Fox.

Shuler Donner, L. (Producer), & Vaughn, M. (Director). (2011). *X-Men: First Class* [Motion picture]. United States: 20th Century Fox.

Weintraub, J. (Producer), & Soderbergh, S. (Director). (2001). *Ocean's Eleven* [Motion picture]. United States: Warner Bros. Pictures.

Commodifying Celebrity: Social media, sensationalism, and how the media plays a role in creating celebrities

Judith Roberts

Abstract: Sensationalism in the media is not new, but the way celebrities and politicians market their persona has changed. Social media has allowed individuals to bypass traditional gatekeepers, and this includes those whose names are commonly in the news. Sensationalised reporting has led to celebrities and politicians making a name for themselves based on their headline-grabbing antics. This chapter looks at the history of sensationalism and focuses on recent and past cases of celebrities in the news and how it has changed over time and discusses how media literacy needs to be implemented to create active citizens who can use and understand new and traditional media.

Keywords: sensationalism, celebrities, social media

Introduction

In the 1900s, sensationalized media in print journalism was used to inform the public about corruption, bribery, and the like. It inflamed the public's spirit to fight for reform. Muckraking and yellow journalism opened doors to sensationalism, partially due to the changes in printing technology, thanks to the Industrial Revolution. Sensationalism began in hopes of attracting readers to newspapers; a competition for readership played out on a national stage as two heavyweights, Hearst, and Pulitzer, fought for readers. A similar change is occurring today with stiff competition among media outlets as the digital age expands the definition of media, journalism, and even reporting. All major media outlets use social media, and even individual journalists are often encouraged to increase readership through their personal social media accounts. Peterson (1981) has posited that "if the press were to serve man well, it [has] to be kept free from all outside control" (p. 13). While he was referring to government restraints, the same can be applied to the media's desire to feed people's hunger for instant gratification and notification, especially when looking at celebrities and how they are covered by the media. Those covered by the news, whether celebrity, politician, or news figures, are often covered with stories full of scandal and intrigue, and the idea of who is a celebrity and who is not, has broadened in definition as technology and public engages in debate of the merits of sensationalized media and how the media commodifies celebrities.

History of Sensationalism

Sensationalism began in the early 19th and 20th centuries with the feud between publishers Joseph Pulitzer and William Randolph Hearst, whose circulation wars led to fat omnibus newspapers. The papers, produced in inexpensively equipped plants with huge payrolls and other business problems, gave way to startling stories. Pulitzer focused on writing and production techniques that set a revolutionary newspaper standard. Not only was his production revolutionary, but so was the writing within the pages. Reporter Elizabeth Cochran, known as Nellie Bly, feigned insanity in order to be committed to Blackwell's Island and then wrote a series of articles that stunned the world. Other reporters on Pulitzer's staff ripped into inhumane prison conditions, cheating tenement builders, greedy monopolists, and aldermen who traded streetcar franchises for bribes (Edwards, 1970).

Similar gatekeeping tendencies can be seen today. The mass media is a business seeking profit, and therefore, economic pressures can contribute as to what is publicized. Competition with media, whether print, online or broadcast, can also affect what is distributed. Also, some owners are cautious and unwilling to stir controversy. Other times, media can be affected by tradition – for example, a general publication may decide something is newsworthy while a public service journalism outlet may decide the information is not necessary to distribute to its audience. The audience always plays a role. Media survive because of the audience. Therefore, the media will print what the audience desires (Mencher, 2003). For example, *The New York Post* will emphasize news dealing with crime, sex, and sports rather than financial or political news, as *The New York Times* stresses, because the *Times'* audience is generally wealthier, better educated, and more interested in politics, the economy, and foreign affairs than the *Post's* audience (Bender, Davenport, Drager, and Fedler, 2012). However, with the rise of social media, gatekeeping by the media has changed from what the media wanted the public to see what the public demands to see.

Recent Research

While many social media tools, such as Facebook, Instagram, or Twitter, offer techniques to users to discuss their favorite books, movies, and hobbies, these social media outlets also can be an informative communication tool for users to discuss any news event at any age, anytime, or any place. By seeing how Twitter, in particular, sparked revolts in Egypt in early 2011, united Americans in the Occupy Wall Street Movement in the fall of the same year, and fostered worldwide assistance after the Japanese earthquake and tsunami in March 2011, micro-blogging encourages macro-reactions. Similarly, when the Penn State scandal broke in November 2011, assistant football coach Jerry Sandusky was found guilty of child molestation and former head football coach Joe Paterno died January 2012, social media activists took to their computers and cell phones to share news stories or post their own thoughts on the situation and asking for others' opinions (Wood, 2012). It was a virtual community connected despite distance to discuss an event, which they could read about, view pictures and videos, and most importantly, post their own comments on the news. More than half of Twitter users share links to news stories, and, of that half, about one-tenth do this at least once a day (Smith & Rainie, 2010). Some social media outlets, such as MySpace, launched in 2003, have reached its peak and are on the decline (Smith, 2015).

Others, like Facebook, which launched a year later, have yet to reach its peak. In August 2015, Facebook had one billion users active on one single day (Wattles, 2015). As of that same month, the social media giant has 1.49 billion monthly active users (statistia.com, 2015). For comparison's sake, Twitter, launched in 2006, has 304 million monthly active users (Lobosco, 2015), and Instagram, a growing photo social media site, has 300 million monthly active users (Protalinski, 2014). The Pew Center has conducted several studies related to Twitter and other forms of social media, attempting to determine who uses social media sites and for what purpose. Hampton, Goulet, Rainie, & Purcell (2011) suggested that the amount one spends on social media sites even varied; for example, 52 percent of Facebook users log in on a daily basis, but only 33 percent of Twitter users accessed their account daily. However, in the same study, Twitter has experienced the highest rate of growth in new members among social networking sites. Madden & Zickuhr (2011) reported more than half of all adults use social networking sites, and 43 percent of adults who use the Internet regularly log into their social networking accounts daily. Young adults are still the most dominant users of social networking sites. But, older age groups have seen faster growth in recent years in that 33 percent of individuals 65 years of age or older has grown from 13 percent in 2009 to 33 percent in 2011 (Madden & Zickuhr, 2011).

One can see how sensationalism can even drive politics and celebrity commodification today. The significance of President Barack Obama's campaign in 2008 should be regarded as one of the most successful, both in terms of voter appeal and fundraising activities, in the United States history. His online campaign, which constituted of social networking sites as well as an easily-accessible web page, helped Obama and his camp circumvent mainstream media in hopes of avoiding gatekeeper tendencies of such media and connecting quicker and with personal appeal than traditional media.

Obama's campaign was more than successful; it was groundbreaking in several instances. One example is his use of new media, which generated increased campaign funds and his prominence on dominant forms of media as well as new media, such as the Internet on sites such as digg.com, MySpace, YouTube, and Facebook. Because of this online campaigning, Obama was able to increase political interest with younger voters, collecting millions of e-mail addresses and other details about donors and volunteers. Bypassing the mainstream media, Obama's camp sent hundreds of e-mails and text messages to its immense number of volunteers and supporters to increase awareness, popularity, and funding. The president's user-friendly Web site served as a platform for the campaign's grassroots activities, which allowed those in the database system to be immediately made aware of distributed press releases, notices of policy positions, and footage of events. Political experts even predicted that Obama's "wired" supporters could be tapped in the future as a possibly lobbying force for the new president's initiatives or endorse candidates nationwide (Obama presidency will be 'wired,' 2009).

The United States presidential election slated in 2016 to replace Obama already has been in the front of the news reports and social media. In August 2015, Donald Trump, a billionaire with no history of holding a government office, was leading the Republican polls. He has switched political parties, he has never held a government office, and he has made demeaning remarks toward women (Murray, 2015; Cabaniss, 2015). However, he stayed in the headlines and in the polls. Part of this reason could be because he is a persona. He's a celebrity. It's not just about what a candidate's policies are. A candidate needs to be entertaining as well.

Celebrities themselves are capitalistic commodities, and the study of celebrities is growing industry. These ordinary people are transformed into something that is seen as extraordinary by the media and public. Celebrity status develops quickly and decays even faster; depending on the revenue the celebrity exhibits. Gossip columns, fan club newsletters, and entertainment magazines offer intimate details about the lives of celebrities, from what their favorite beverages are to where they went on vacation. No detail is too private, no scandal too horrific for the public and paparazzi. Even celebrities from earlier decades live on through reruns, "classic" movies, and oldie radio stations. Those who die young are often transformed into cultural icons, though generally, celebrity decays with age (Kurzman, Anderson, Key, Lee, Moloney, Silver, Van Ryn, 2007). Franck and Nuesch (2007) stated that there are two types of celebrities: self-made superstars and manufactured celebrities. The self-made stars are the ones such as Placido Domingo or Michael Jordan, who are considered among the most talented in their field. Media provide access to these types of superstars in various ways, such as broadcasting a sports competition or airing an interview with a designer. On the other hand, manufactured celebrities can be seen on shows such as *Big Brother, Keeping up with the Kardashians,* and *America's Next Top Model.* The mass media artificially creates these celebrities through publicity and promotion. Recent technological advances in communication with the Internet and social media have also created pseudo-celebrities out of anyone with an Internet connection. Technological improvements have allowed celebrities to become more visible than ever before and allowed a new type of celebrity to emerge: a trivial celebrity who is simply well known for being, pun intended, well-known. This is not necessarily a new technique, just one that has been created from new tools, such as the Internet Technology has been used to further one's celebrity status since television. In the 1950s, for example, television quiz shows were ways for celebrities to garner attention (Nüesch, 2007). At any rate, visibility allows celebrities to reach a pinnacle of professional success. While the general public may still believe that celebrities are discovered for their natural abilities, talent is only one component to the puzzle. Media and other channels also must be present to deliver the celebrities to the audience (Rein, Kotler, and Stoller, 1997).

Celebrities, of course, can also be politicians. Political figureheads, from a village mayor to the president of the United States, are being sensationalized, over-hyped media fodder. The media often focus more on conflict rather than compromise when it comes to politics. Due to the series of high-profile abuses of power in the 1990s, researchers have started to believe that the coverage of political figures has begun to slip into a spiral of sensationalism (Morris & Clawson, 2005). The question now is whether or not this is damaging for the politics of the country: if so, it would be logical for the politicians in scandals or sensationalized stories to remove themselves from tales of scandal to keep their jobs. Most politicians do use social media for campaigning. Trump and many other 2016 presidential hopefuls use their social media feed to grow their popularity. For example, Republican Jeb Bush and Democrat Hillary Clinton used Twitter to its fullest extent in August 2015, posting pointed barbs, graphics, and muddled facts to argue their point on higher education and taxes – and this was before the Republican or Democratic presidential nominee was ever announced (Makarechi, 2015). Even though most, if not all, of the presidential hopefuls experienced scandal, they came through unscathed, often through social media. As noted with Twitter power rankings following the Bengazi hearings, Clinton's tweets were still the most retweeted and favorite of the week of the hearings (Voorhees and Kahn, 2015). Perhaps, based on this knowledge, sensationalism and news go hand in hand and reinforce each other. The effect continues not only for that individual's popularity but also for the public's overall view of politics and political institutions. Studies have shown that voters expect much more from politicians than politicians do of themselves, which often places upon their shoulders unreasonable expectations. The words Iran-Contra and Lewinsky immediately bring memories of former political scandals to voters' minds. Studies of these scandals reveal a decline of trust in politicians. The democracy in this country experienced a series of high-profile scandals in the 90s, and while politicians would like to blame the media, the real culprits of the decline are politicians themselves (Bowler & Karp, 2004).

The problem with the media is to give life to the role of interpretive reporting, which seems to be a niche of what tabloids have dove. From breaking the story of Jesse Jackson's illegitimate child to catching former President George W. Bush's daughter, Jenna, smoking marijuana, politics is the new story for tabloid due, naturally, to a falling circulation. By blurring the line between sensationalism and politics, media receive what they want – profits – and the public is submerged under a sea of sensationalism. Jenna Bush's smoking antics was news, the tabloid journalists said, because of her father's tough stance on marijuana (Economist, 2001). The trends toward finding sensational stories have persisted. Sensationalism may be a form of entertainment, but celebrities and politicians should not have as much influence in affairs unless they are informed subjects. Also, coverage of private lives of government officials, while sometimes needed, often goes to far. The public may feel they need to be entertained by news, but a journalist's role as media watchdog is to simply report the facts; sensationalism is only an option (Proffitt, 2007). Journalists should adhere to a code of ethics and perhaps omit sensationalistic details. Actions garner reactions, and journalists should remember this. The public should also remember that they are a thesis of change in public policy. Journalists in the field and scholars both agree that sensationalistic reporting is growing at an alarming rate, and the result could be a government elected on sensationalistic reporting and not accolades and accomplishments. Media need to publish information to enlighten democratic citizens and support the public's efforts of self-governance through logical decisions (Slattery, Doremus, and Marcus, 2001). As John Katz (pg. 62, 1999), a media critic for *Wired* magazine, noted, "The most faithful among media watchers have always held that the media don't lead, they follow…If you watch long enough and closely enough, the truth will unfailingly emerge, however indirectly, and often in the most surprising ways."

Conclusion

The media have been traditionally described as the thesis of change, and this is still inherent as politicians and celebrities use the media to garner attention through sensational media and commodifying individuals and ideas.

According to Robin Henry Lee, media, from the beginning of its history, have shaped and directed society and even one's own consciousness. Journalists hold the power to alter a person's perceptions and even create an opinion where none was held before (Lee, 1977). Younger audiences, who have turned away from newspapers, television, and radio in striking numbers, are turning towards more a non-journalistic media they believe is more truthful, and that offers strong points of view and blunt exchanges of ideas, such as an online blog. The ascending media are now Web pages, Hollywood films, Comedy Central programs, MTV News, and such, which make no claim to be objective, comprehensive, or even substantial (Katz, 1999). As Croteau and Hoynes (2001) noted, the public has grown more active with the increased online productivity. With increased media literacy skills and critical analysis skills to understand better the socially constructed nature of the media, hopefully the public can recognize this sensationalism and understand how celebrities and politicians alike use the media to commodify themselves and how the media do the same. Media literacy skills need to be implemented not only in adults, but also for children, and people in turn can understand how the new and traditional media work and what they as active participant citizens can do to change society for the better.

References

Bender, J. R., Davenport, L.D., Drager, M.W., & Fedler, F. (2012). Reporting for the Media. *10th Ed. New York: Oxford University Press.*

Bowler, S. and Karp, J.A. (2004). Politicians, scandals, and trust in government. *Political Behavior, 26*(3).

Cabaniss, W. (2015). Donald Trump says 'he didn't say' the things about women that Megyn Kelly asked him about in debate. *PolitiFact.com.* Retrieved September 28, 2015, from http://www.politifact.com/truth-o-meter/statements/2015/aug/10/donald-trump/donald-trump-says-women-viciously-attacked-him-fir/

Campbell, W. J. (2001). Yellow Journalism: Puncturing the Myths, Defining the Legacies. *Wesport, Conn.: Praeger.*

Cassidy, W. P. (2006). Gatekeeping similar for online, print journalists. *Newspaper Research Council, 27*(2).

Croteau, D. and Hoynes, W. (2001). The Business of Media: Corporate Media and the Public Interest. *Calif.: Pine Forge Press.*

Economist (2001). *Pass the Pulitzers,* 360(8229).

Edwards, V. E. (1970). Journalism in a Free Society. *Ohio Wesleyan University: William C. Brown Co.*

Emery, M. C., & Emery, E. (1996). The Press and America: An Interpretive History of the Mass Media. *8th Ed. Needham Heights, MA*: Simon & Schuster.

Franck, E., & Nuesch, S. (2007). Avoiding 'Star Wars' – Celebrity creation as media strategy. *Kyklos, 60*(2).

Hampton, K. N., Goulet, L. S., Rainie, L., & Purcell, K. (2011). Social networking sites and our lives. *Pew Internet and American Life Project*. Retrieved January 16, 2012, from http://pewinternet.org/~/media//Files/Reports/2011/PIP%20%20Social%20networking%20sites%20and%20our%20lives.pdf.

Haque, M. (2009). Lecture notes from the Media and Culture class.

Katz, J. (1999). Guilty: Objectivity is obsolete. *The Power of the Press*. Ed. Beth Levy and Denise M. Bonilla. New York: H. W. Wilson Company, 1999. 61-72.

Kurzman, C., Anderson, C., Key, C., Lee, Y.O., Moloney, M., Silver, A., & Van Ryn, M. W. (2007). Celebrity status. *Sociological Theory, 25*(4).

Lee, R. H. (1977). Media and change. *Media and Change*. Ed. J.A.F. Van Zyl & K.G. Tomaselli. Johannesburg: McGraw-Hill Book Company.

Lobosco, K. (2015). Twitter still doesn't have as many users as Instagram. *CNNMoney*. Retrieved Sept. 28, 2015, from http://money.cnn.com/2015/02/05/investing/twitter-earnings/users/.

Madden, M. & Zickuhr, K. (2011). 65% of online adults use social networking sites. *Pew Internet and American Life Project*. Retrieved January 16, 2012, from http://www.pewinternet.org/~/media//Files/Reports/2011/PIP-SNS-Update-2011.pdf.

Makarechi, K. (2015). Jeb Bush and Hillary Clinton got into a Twitter fight. *VF News.* Retrieved Nov. 3, 2015, from http://www.vanityfair.com/news/2015/08/jeb-bush-hillary-clinton-twitter-fight.

Mencher, M. (2003). *News Reporting and Writing*. 9th ed. Boston: McGraw-Hill.

Morris, J. S. and Clawson, R.A. (2005). Media coverage of Congress in the 1990s: Scandals, personalities, and the prevalence of policy and process. *Political Communication, 22*(1).

Murray, M. (2015). NBC/WSJ Poll: Trump and Carson Lead GOP; Clinton Loses Ground. *NBC News*. Retrieved Sept. 29, 2015, from http://www.nbcnews.com/meet-the-press/nbc-wsj-poll-2016-goprace-n433991.

Nüesch, S. (2007). Different Star Strategies in the Media — Why "Manufactured" Celebrities are More Lucrative than "Self-Made" Superstars. *The Economics of Superstars and Celebrities.* Gabler.

Obama Presidency will be 'Wired.' (2009). *Information Management Journal* (43)1, 7. Retrieved September 27, 2015, from EBSCOhost database.

Peterson, T. (1981). Mass media and their environments: A journey into the past. *What's news?* Ed. Elie Abel. San Francisco: Institute for Contemporary Studies.

Proffitt, J. M. (2007). Challenges to Democratic Discourse: Media Concentration and the Marginalization of Dissent. *Review of Education, Pedagogy, and Cultural Studies 29(*1).

Protalinski, E. (2014). Facebook passes 1.23 billion monthly active users, 945 million mobile users, and 757 million daily users. *TNW News*. Retrieved Sept. 28, 2015, from http://thenextweb.com/facebook/2014/01/29/facebook-passes-1-23-billion-monthly-active-users-945-million-mobile-users-757-million-daily-users/.

Rein, I., Kotler, P., & Stoller, M. (1997). *High Visibility: The making and marketing of professionals into celebrities.* Lincolnwood, IL: NTC Business Books.

Statistica.com (2015). Number of monthly active Facebook users worldwide as of 2nd quarter 2015 (in millions). Retrieved Sept. 28, 2015, from http://www.statista.com/statistics/264810/number-of-monthly-active-facebook-users-worldwide/.

Slattery, K., Doremus, M., & Marcus, L. (2001). Shifts in public affairs reporting on the network evening news: A move toward the sensational. *Journal of Broadcasting and Electronic Media, 45*(2).

Smith, A., & Rainie, L. (2010). Who tweets? *Pew Internet & American Life Project.* Retrieved November 1, 2015, from http://pewresearch.org/pubs/1821/twitter-users-profile-exclusive-examination.

Smith, C. (2015). By the numbers: 17 MySpace Stats and Facts then and now. Retrieved Sept.28, 2015, from http://expandedramblings.com/index.php/myspace-stats-then-now/.

Voorhes, J. and Kahn, A. (2015). This week's 2016 Twitter Power Rankings. Slate. Retrieved November 3, 2015, from http://www.slate.com/blogs/the_slatest/2015/10/30/hillary_clinton_donald_trump_win_twitter_power_rankings.html.

Wattles, J. (2015). Facebook hits one billion users in a single day. *CNNMoney*. Retrieved Sept. 28, 2015, from http://money.cnn.com/2015/08/27/technology/facebook-one-billion-users-single-day/.

Wood, D. (2012). Joe Paterno: Twitter mourns passing of coaching legend. *Bleacher Report*. Retrieved September 25, 2015, from http://bleacherreport.com/articles/1034068-joe-paterno-twitter-mourns-passing-of-coaching-legend.

Quantifying Celebrity: Influence Measurement in the Digital Age

Andrew Zolides

Abstract. We live in the age of the codified self with the massive growth of digital technologies used to track, broadcast, and quantify our lives. When one can (questionably) measure such previously imprecise subjective markers like social influence, taste, and - most importantly for celebrities – fame, those understandings cycle back into the way identity is performed and reported on within these digital spaces. I explore this quantification of fame markers through the case study of Klout and its relationship to previous attempts at quantifying popularity, namely the Q Score. These metrics are an attempt to create an economy of influence that can be translated into the fiscal economy but open to any individual with a social media account. Understanding the Q Score and related metrics like Nielsen's recent attempts at branching out into social media serve as a useful entry point into the world of quantifying 'celebrity,' as marketers shift away from a focus on audience size and towards more abstract concepts like engagement. Digitization leads to an increased reliance upon and expectation of codifiable measurements, even those of seemingly subjective concepts like popularity and influence. This connects to an increased commodification, as the creation of multiple systems of value mean new relationships are forming within each. This has huge stakes for culture and celebrity journalism industries that are heavily invested in the promotion and commodification of personas and related media texts.

Keywords: quantification; fame; celebrity; social media; big data

Introduction

Digitization has had an impact on nearly all sectors of the media economy, including the celebrity commodity industry. The ability to digitally measure a celebrity's possible value to an advertiser means a new conception of what the celebrity commodity actual is and how it can best be produced. Most importantly, digital tools of convergence have led to an expansion of celebrity-based marketing tactics that involve non-traditional celebrities, encouraging everyone to create their own audiences and celebrity personas. Now celebrity status is not limited to those who work in the media industries. Everyone is able to create a sensational celebrity commodity and the audience that comes with it, leading to value in an economy that rewards and encourages everyone to build their own audiences through social media.

This chapter explores the industry of quantifying fame markers like influence in the digital age while comparing it to earlier attempts. Services like Q-Scores and Klout attempt to create what I term an *influence economy* that can be translated into a fiscal economy and is open to any individual with a social media account. Convergence has blurred the lines between traditional and non-traditional celebrity. Now new industries are emerging to take advantage of these understandings. In the influence economy, anyone can make money for the audience they generate.

The Influence Economy

The celebrity industry and its modern corollaries are built upon an *influence economy*. The term is derived from popular discourse within the marketing sector that refers to 'influencers' and 'influencer marketing' as trends and strategies for approaching various branding practices. This concept is not necessarily a new one, but it is certainly more important now and increasingly more utilized in discourse when it applies to online performances of the self and their commercialization. The idea of using influence as the basis for a marketing strategy dates back to the 1940s, as sociologists Paul Lazarsfeld and Elihu Katz published books like *The People's Choice* (1944) and *Personal Influence* (1955). Their research showed the greater power of influencing through one's personal network versus broadcasting stating, "their coverage is greater, and they have certain psychological advantages over the formal media" (Lazarsfeld et. al., 1944, pg. 150). Although focusing on how political decisions are made, this research would form the foundation for a new perspective in marketing based on utilizing people's social networks, something that has only become more pronounced in the age of digital social media.

I argue for a new focus and understanding on this idea of an *influence economy* and the *labor of influence* upon which it is built. Microcelebrities (Internet-based stars), celebrities, and brands' use of social media and the businesses that have emerged to support them indicate an economic system whose primary site of valuation comes from the idea of 'influence.' This new paradigm for doing business expands on ideas of the audience engagement and persuasion in an update of traditional marketing. By approaching the growing use of online social media by mass and niche celebrities as an influence economy, we can better understand the ways industries emerge to support such work. One of those industries is the focus of this article: the influence measurement firm.

Celebrity Studies' Blindspot

There is a blindspot in our approach to the celebrity industry, and it is similar to one addressed years ago in the study of television. Dallas Smythe and

Graham Murdock pushed for an academic shift in studying the television industry towards the audience commodity, a move often referred to as the 'Blindspot Debate.' Essentially, their work argued that the true commodity produced in the television industry was not television content but the audiences that watched it. Foundational to the study of the television industry, the question of the audience commodity is pushed further with Eileen Meehan considering the role of rating firms. Serving as an intermediary between the television networks and potential clients – advertisers – rating companies like Nielsen serve a powerful function in the television economy. As Meehan (1984) notes, "the process of translating viewers into a verified audience – that is, into ratings – remains peculiarly aloof from the constraints and pressures that shape all other forms of commodity production in capitalism" (p. 221). Put simply, one must understand the process of this rating-generating function if one is to engage truly with the television industry. The political economies of these companies remind us that ratings are not a science; they are a business.

This audience-commodity blindspot is also present in the field of celebrity studies. We must ask ourselves how the celebrity industry is one that generates audiences (of celebrities) instead of just celebrity personas. Given this, how are those audiences measured and valued? The answer to this question has of course changed over time. Before considering how celebrity is measured in the digital age, early fame measuring services provided a foundation for quantifying and evaluating celebrities for all their industrial purposes.

Q-Scores: The Original Fame Metric

Founded in 1964, Marketing Evaluations Inc. has continued to generate the venerable Q-Score in much the same old-fashioned approach it has since the beginning. The process begins with questionnaires physically mailed to people across the United States with a constantly updated membership. In this way, Q-Scores fit closely to Nielsen's traditional system of surveys and viewing booklets. Yet Nielsen has also expanded in recent years to include more automatic measurements through tracking boxes and social media metrics. The Q-Score surveys begin by asking people some personal demographic information that helps Marketing Evaluations break down their data by various groups – once again showing the importance of the 'audience commodity' in play with these measurements. Marketing Evaluations purposely keeps this system low-key and under the radar. As president Steven Levitt described in a 1992 *New York Times* article, he doesn't want the public to be necessarily aware of Q-Scores for performers since that knowledge could impact their opinions on that performer "perhaps expecting more than before" (Finkle, 1992). This position speaks both to Marketing Evaluations' method of data collection and the difficulty of taking a proper measurement of something as subjective and malleable as popularity. Fame is a socially formed attribute, so it is thus susceptible to social influence itself. It is for this reason Marketing Evaluations' is in a difficult position of making its measurements both marketable and accurate, two goals that can come into conflict. The data Marketing Evaluations generates is then sold to a variety of media industries such as advertising agencies, public relations firms, production companies, networks, casting directors, talent and their representation, and a whole host of other institutions invested - both literally and figuratively - in the supposed popularity of famous personas. The Q-Score becomes a currency within the celebrity ecosystem for cost-analysis, risk-assessment, and negotiated wages. Essentially, Q-Scores look to assign market value to human beings for their exchange throughout the media industries.

Yet what exactly is a Q-Score measuring if it is meant to have such wide-ranging effects? The surveys are surprisingly brief, usually asking just two primary questions in regards to its list of public figures both fictional and across the realm of media, sports, and branding. The first question asks if the survey-taker has heard of the person, followed by the second question which asks how that person would be 'rated' on a scale from poor to "one of your favorites." In sum, Q-Scores measure just two features: familiarity and likeability, as the Q-Score itself indicates the percentage of people listing someone as one of their favorites divided by the percentage that recognize the name. The Q-Score, then, is measuring how well-liked a celebrity is amongst the people who actually know him or her.

These two measurements actually provide a relatively nuanced understanding of a celebrity's possible value to a third party. Q-Scores can tell you how familiar the public is with a person as well as if that familiarity is generally positive. This means a relatively little-known celebrity might have a high Q-Score if those who do know him or her are generally fond of that person. This is important when making decisions in terms of narrowcasting and niche-targeting with brands. While the sheer size of one's potential audience is of course still important, a small but dedicated following certainly obtains a certain level of value because of its potential to actually have a positive connection with the persona involved, increasing the likelihood of consumer action (seeing a film, buying a product, watching an appearance, etc.) in response. What might seem at first glance a shockingly simplistic system actually proves much deeper than expected.

The Q-Score's focus on familiarity and likeability provides a solid foundation to investigate the current rise of the *influence economy*. While the

Q-Score is unable to provide answers to how influential a potential celebrity could be, Marketing Evaluations is attempting to use the valuation of familiarity and likability as a stand-in/predictor of possible influence. This follows a commonsense logic that someone known and liked would be more likely to influence potential audiences than one missing either trait. Despite the lack of direct reference to influence, the idea of using numbers to indicate these characteristics is still utilized today, through frequently in different forms. Consider the YouTube measurements of views, subscriptions and likes or 'thumbs-up.' The first two measures are in some ways a gathering of the actual total audience and the latter two speak to the positive association with that video. All of these measures, of course, have their own issues with data gathering and application, as context, reception, and diversity are not perfectly represented here just as they are not in the Q-Score. What does remain is the idea that measuring how well-known and how positively perceived a person is acts as a suitable indicator – at least to those in the industry – of success in the *influence economy* built upon the notion of creating and selling an audience commodity.

Measurements for a Digital Age

While Q-Scores are still around, there has been recent growth in utilizing digital analytics to generate measurements in 'social influence' derived primarily from social media websites. One of the fascinating results of this shift to digital measurement is a broadening of the celebrity rating to those people and entities we might not consider traditional celebrities. One of the inherent limitations of the Q-Score survey method is how the people and brands to be measured are chosen. Marketing Evaluations must generate a list in the first place, thus performing a crucial step in the choosing of who even 'counts' enough to be measured. Digital ratings services and algorithms open up that context, reworking the traditional economic system and allowing more producer input over the measurement of his or her own self-brand. Put in a larger context, we see the effects of what Henry Jenkins calls *convergence culture* in the world of celebrity (Jenkins 2006). One of the results of the broad convergence of media technologies, cultures, and audiences is the blurring of the distinction between producer and consumer. The Web and other digital tools have created fewer financial, institutional, and intellectual barriers to entry not just for mass production by individuals but also mass distribution. "Once you have a reliable system of distribution, folk culture production begins to flourish again overnight" (Jenkins, 2006, pg. 140). Indeed, convergence leads to a blurring of producer and consumer identities wherein more people are able to create cultural content, including individual personas.

What this means for the celebrity industry is similar to what it means for other media industries: more people can create media content. For the celebrity industry, it means that new celebrities can emerge from the realm of what used to be restricted from those outside the industry positioned as mere consumers. This has been documented most notably by the rise of micro-celebrities and Internet stars as a new cultural formation and a new line of celebrity labor and production (Senft, 2008, Hearn, 2008, Marwick, 2013). Yet we need not even limit our examination to the rise of a new category of Internet-based celebrities, but question what happens when the tools of celebrity measurement are provided to the public at large. Klout is an online digital reputation site offering tools to individuals and corporations to measure their online 'social influence' through the tracking of their social media activity. This shows the blurring going on in the *influence economy* where individuals are taking cues from corporations in the application of branding practices and corporations are learning from individuals by applying tools of social media to their larger marketing strategies. Social influence and its measurement come down to the valuation (and thus monetization) of social media activity with tools now made available to anyone with a social media account and the drive to measure oneself. Through looking at the business and discourse surrounding digital social influence websites, the *influence economy* reveals new avenues for generating value and transferring social capital into financial capital.

Klout

Launched in 2008 Klout measures "online impact" using a hidden proprietary algorithm that uses one's social media activity to generate a Klout Score between 1 and 100. While the algorithm is not public, the measurement is based on various elements: the type of content shared/generated, the size of the network seeing and engaging with that content, the type of engagement that audience is performing (e.g. retweets, favoriting, sharing, liking, etc.), and perhaps most importantly the relative influence of those people within one's network. The data is pulled from any social network accounts the user chooses to include in the calculation. This algorithm shows the values Klout embodies from the *influence economy*. As the algorithm breakdown makes clear, it is not just one's own content that matters or even the reach of one's message; rather, it is the influence, and relative value of one's *audience* that grants one a higher Klout score, as those who engage with your content are only as valuable as the audience they, in turn, can reach. This last point is made even clearer by Klout's own website stating, "We believe it's better to have a small and engaged audience than a large network that doesn't respond to your content." To put it simply, your social influence is only as good as your audience's.

This relates to the contemporary *influence economy* and celebrity industry in a myriad of ways. Firstly, the value is seen as coming primarily from one's audience, not one's message or content. As the name suggests, the *influence economy* values influence over all else, and that influence necessarily demands an audience willing and able to receive one's messages. Next, the twin markers of familiarity and likeability emerge again, as the size of one's potential audience is only one portion of the value calculation. Indeed, it is the positive connection with that audience that attributes value to the individual. The primary difference between the digitalscape of sites like Klout versus the more old-fashioned Q-Score is how one determines those positive associations. Instead of surveys, digital services utilize data in the form of 'engagements' to determine those factors. This makes sense, as those engagements become new distribution avenues in their own right, extending the spreadability of the content and thus its value. Lastly, the emphasis on small yet engaged audiences echoes the shifts in contemporary media narrowcasting and niche-marketing, wherein the audience's value comes more from its loyalty and possible demographic make-up than its supposed size. Data derived digitally can allow for more nuance and specificity that marketers view as necessary in an age of personalized media consumption. When people turn to a wider variety of sources for their media, the quality of those connections becomes a stronger choice in getting consumer's attention versus the quantity of messages seen.

Klout has itself been the source of criticism and social commentary which can be seen as the culture responding to these shifting economic understandings of social media activity. Critiques of Klout often fall into either a questioning of its opaque methodology or a broader cynicism of its role in society. While Klout can and has more easily addressed the former criticism through updating its algorithm by including broader web data, the latter point reaches to the heart of what Klout represents and speaks to the larger skepticism and paradoxical relationship the broader culture has with the notion of a 'quantified self.' David Berry (2012) describes the quantified self-movement saying, "this kind of self-collection of data is certainly becoming more prevalent and in the context of reflexivity and self-knowledge, it raises interesting questions about the increasing use of mathematics and computation to understand and control the self." Klout goes a measure beyond this self-reflexivity and opens up the possibility of engaging third parties in an economic exchange of valuable goods and services. We're no longer just expressing ourselves online; we're building brands. It is for this reason Klout is referred to as everything from innovative to evil (Scalzi, 2011), perhaps receiving its harshest indictment from Charlie Stross who called it "the internet equivalent of herpes" (Stross, 2011). There is resistance to the notion that one could or would even wish to reduce something as personal and subjective as 'influence' to a number, not to mention the skepticism over whether it could even be done with any sense of accurately reflecting reality.

I do not wish to weigh in on whether Klout and services like it are any good, accurate, or the wave of the future though it is worth pointing out Klout was purchased for $200 million by Lithium Technologies in March 2014. What is important to take away from Klout's existence and the discourse surrounding it is the notion of the branded self it advances. The drive for a Klout score is similar to any drive for social relevancy, but the quantification it provides encourages individuals to take on particular branding strategies, not unlike those undertaken by major corporations and advertising firms. This push for branded individualism falls in line with larger neoliberal trends in the today's precarious, freelance project-based economy. This is important for our understanding of celebrity and celebrity is important for our understanding of this phenomenon because celebrities are the original branded individuals.

Conclusion: Celebrity Convergence

The growth of data mining for the benefit of valuing celebrities and other online public figures has dual effects of encouraging new strategies for traditional celebrities and opening up new avenues for non-traditional internet celebrities to emerge. There can be no question that big data makes big news, as trade and popular press constantly reference the importance of using numbers to make crucial industrial decisions like which star to cast or which public figure to sign as a spokesperson for a brand or product. Yet we should remember that this in itself does not prove these numbers to be any more reliable in predicting success in the market. Rather, numbers are a *perceived* as more reliable by those within the industry. For the worker making these choices, it is much more prudent to cite numbers as the reason behind a bad decision than one's own 'bad instinct.'

These celebrity quantification services also support an *influence economy* and influencer marketing models. When everyone is able to generate an audience through a variety of social media networks, suddenly everyone is a potential endorser. Celebrities were traditionally considered the primary mode of reaching a new audience through a personal (or para-social) connection; however the convergence of media technologies and the blurring of the producer/consumer divide has led to new options for advertisers to spread their message. Anyone with a social media account and an audience is a laborer in the *influence economy*. Data analytic companies serve the significant role of generating the currency of exchange that values that labor, the individual personas behind them, and those audiences who follow. For celebrities this means we must broaden our research and understandings to find connections between traditional and non-traditional trends. Rather than sequestering the concept of 'celebrity' to its own special category of person, it is more useful to expand its reach to consider all those who labor towards the construction of a valuable, spectacular commodity-persona. Social media is the primary site for these new formations, so we must also understand the political economies and technologies underlying these services to consider what strategies and activities they do and do not enable.

References

Berry, D. (2012) *Life in Code and Software: Mediated Life in a Complex Computational Ecology*. Open Humanities Press.

Finkle, D. (1992, June 7). Q Ratings: The Popularity of the Stars. *The New York Times*. http://www.nytimes.com/1992/06/07/arts/television-q-ratings-the-popularity-contest-of-the-stars.html.

Hearn, A. (2008) "Meat Mask Burden": Probing the Contours of the Branded Self. *Journal of Consumer Culture*, 8(2), 197-217. doi:10.1177/1469540508090086

Jenkins, H. (2006). *Convergence Culture: Where Old and New Media Collide*. New York, NY: New York UP.

Katz, E., & Lazarsfeld, P. F. (1955). *Personal Influence: The Part Played by People in the Flow of Mass Communications*. New York, NY: The Free Press.

Lazarsfeld, P. F., Berelson, B., & Gaudet, H. (1944). *People's Choice: How the Voter Makes up His Mind in a Presidential Campaign*. New York, NY: Columbia UP.

Marwick, A. (2013) *Status Update: Celebrity, Publicity, and Branding in the Social Media Age*. New Haven, CT: Yale UP.

Meehan, E. (1984). Ratings and the Institutional Approach: A Third Answer to the Commodity Question. *Critical Studies in Mass Communication*, 1(2), 216-225. doi:10.1080/15295038409360032.

Scalzi, J. (2011, November 15) Why Klout Scores Are Possibly Evil. *CNN Money*. http://money.cnn.com/2011/11/15/technology/klout_scores/.

Senft, T. (2008) *Camgirls: Celebrity and Community in the Age of Social Networks*. New York, NY: Lang.

Stross, C. (2011, November 7). Evil Social Networks. *Antipope*. http://www.antipope.org/charlie/blog-static/2011/11/evil-social-networks.html.

PART III

Bridging Media Controversy and Celebrity Status

A Persona of Global Controversy: Assange, Snowden, and the Makings of the Digital Information Activist

Andrew Munro

Abstract. This chapter examines two controversial celebrities: ex-hacker and editor of the whistleblowing platform WikiLeaks, Julian Assange, and the former U.S. National Security Agency contractor who leaked a trove of classified documents concerning state mass surveillance programs, Edward Snowden. I read Assange and Snowden as two related but contrastive performances of a contemporary persona: the celebrity digital information activist. By *persona*, I mean a speaking position emergent from and responsive to a series of institutional constraints and social practices, a kind of person or character established through repeated discursive use. By *performance*, I mean both the collaborations and conflicts of Assange and Snowden with the mainstream press, and the range of biographical interventions by journalists that take Assange and Snowden as their objects of inquiry. I argue that the performances of Assange and Snowden—their actions and the mediatic reception of these last as achievements and missteps—comprise two key contributions to the ongoing, ethopoetical construction of the persona of the digital information activist.

Keywords: persona; information activism; whistleblowing; rhetoric; genre.

Rhetorical Personae

In this chapter, I will signal some of the heuristic potential of *persona* for celebrity and media studies. In particular, I will present persona as a tool that enables us to engage with contemporary controversies concerning digital information and digital information activism. Evidently, interest in persona as an analytic postulate is enjoying a welcome resurgence today (Marshall, 2014; Marshall, Moore & Barbour, 2015). A risk associated with this rediscovery, however, is that we end up wielding persona as a pretty blunt instrument. In what follows, I suggest that we sharpen the persona in our methodological toolkit by construing this notion rhetorically.

On this account, persona sorts with the postulates of public relations, folk psychology, semiotics and rhetoric. Focused on neither celebrity commodification nor fantasies of sovereign star agency, persona is a product of *ethopoeia*: the performative, discursive construction of full human character (Miller, 2001). Persona in this sense denotes a speaking position in process, a *kind of person* (Hacking, 1995; 2001) or *character* never fully settled, established through and inflected by repeated discursive use (Fowler, 2003; Frow, 2006). We can thus take persona as something of a sensitizing concept (Driessens, 2015): we posit a discursive phenomenon—here, the persona of the celebrity digital information activist—in order to attend to some of its varied expressions in particular contexts—in this instance, the contrastive performances of Julian Assange and Edward Snowden. Put otherwise, persona helps us to apprehend a socio-discursive scene (Woo, Rennie & Poyntz, 2015) or sphere of activity: here, we read the celebrity digital information activist as an enabling persona of digital leaking.

Mediating Biographies

To position this persona, I will focus on two objects of recent media copy, and one generic instrument by means of which these objects are being made and taken up. The two objects are the aforementioned stars of the universe of digital information activism: ex-hacker and editor-in-chief of the whistleblowing platform WikiLeaks, Julian Assange, and the former U.S. National Security Agency (NSA) contractor who leaked a trove of classified documents, Edward Snowden. The generic instrument is biography, or rather, interventions in a broadly biographical mode.

The range of such interventions taking Assange and Snowden as object indicates the polarizing power of these two figures, and contributes to how their star status is attributed and achieved. In the case of Assange, biographical outputs range from accounts of his juvenile hacking exploits to memoirs of disgruntled former colleagues, from cypherpunk manifestoes to book-length assessments of the achievements of Assange and WikiLeaks, from fictionalized spy-thrillers to an official but unauthorized autobiography.[1] In the case of Snowden, we count comics, graphic novels, novelizations, colleagues' insider accounts, denunciatory e-books, documentaries and upcoming films.[2] In both cases and all instances—from interviews and profile pieces to insider memoirs, documentaries and biopics—the biographical mode does significant rhetorical work. Certainly, by storying these individuals' lives, biographical inquiry frames Assange and Snowden as persons, intentional moral agents subsisting over discursive spheres, time and space. But by positioning their actions variously as achievements and missteps,

---

[1] See, for example, Assange, Appelbaum, Müller-Maguhm and Zimmerman (2012); Assange and O'Hagan (2013); Condon (2013); Domscheit-Berg 2011; Dreyfus 2001; Fowler (2011); Gibney (2013); Greenberg (2012); Leigh and Harding (2011); Star (2011). Laura Poitras's *Asylum* documentary is showcasing at the 2015 New York Film festival.

[2] See, for example, D'Orazio (2014); Greenwald (2014); Harding (2014); Lucas (2014); Poitras (2014); Rall (2015). Oliver Stone's *Snowden*, based on Harding's (2014) *The Snowden Files*, is due for release in 2016.

biographical inquiry also promotes Assange and Snowden as performances of the persona of the digital information activist. Biography, like leaking, is both a mediated and mediating activity.

Trust, Anonymity, Publicity, Controversy

Plainly, many actors shape the global rhetorical public spheres that are currently debating information and press freedoms and institutional accountability. Many moments and situations, similarly, make up digital leaking's ecologies. Notable among these is a post 9/11 environment of mass secret making, secret sharing and secret taking, a culture enabled and constrained by the anonymizing affordances of encryption and the distributive capacities of the internet. Overlapping offices—from whistleblowers and digital technicians to legal representatives, public advocates, and the mainstream or legacy press— are also critical enablers of digital leaking.

In this respect, the press is pivotal not only to selecting, framing and disseminating data leaked, but also to constituting the speaking position, or making up the persona, of the digital information activist. In large swathes of the mainstream media, the figures of Assange and Snowden are frequently defined by means of intertextually-charged hyperbole. Assange, we learn, has eclipsed Daniel Ellsberg to become "the most dangerous man in the world", while Snowden is suddenly the "world's most wanted".[3] These epithets and descriptions are then often glossed, but rarely problematized, as dichotomies: information messiah or cyberterrorist, dissenter and principled patriot or traitor and fame-seeking narcissist. Pervading these tales, too, is a surveillance spy thematic. The cloak-and-dagger content—the bullet proof vests and encryption keys, the talk of burner phones, honeytraps and intercepts— doubtless makes for intriguing copy.

A commercial imperative, however, is surely not the sole driver of journalistic coverage of these cases. In a pressingly pragmatic sense, the figures of Assange and Snowden speak to the very office of the press. Whether a leaker is lauded, lambasted or ignored, depends partly on how mainstream journalism self-presents: how legacy media outlets discharge their duties in relation to transjurisdictional new media players like WikiLeaks, and how they assume or abdicate the watchdog role associated with the fourth estate (Brevini, Hintz & McCurdy, 2013).

---

[3] See, for example, the book-length treatments by journalists such as Fowler (2011) and Harding (2014).

But whether framing Assange and Snowden as cyberterrorists and traitors or crediting them with raising timely questions about internet freedom and the national security state, the tales of journalists are inextricably tied to the storying of the lives of leakers and the ascription to these last of diverse motives and intents. Pragmatically and rhetorically, the figures and fortunes of Assange and Snowden show digital leaking to be not merely a matter of information flows and onion rings: the public revelation—and reception—of sensitive state information is constitutively tied to the performance of a persona, a rhetorical management of face (Munro, 2015).

In this regard, mass digital leaking fundamentally resembles its analogue equivalent. Both of these enterprises, after all, are rhetorically grounded in a mediagenic performance of persona and a capital of trust. Initially, the self-presentation of the whistle-blower turns on the assertion of a moral imperative: a radical loss of trust in the state is advanced as compelling grounds for whistleblowing. However, for the whistleblower's claims to gain public traction, this performance of mistrust must in turn translate to a trust instilled in the whistleblower and in the publishing leaker for whom the whistleblower is the source. The reason for this is simple: we value information in relation to the ethos—the character capital, credibility or authority—that we assign to the information's source.

The state well understands this truism of public relations, semiotics and rhetoric: recall President Richard Nixon's warrantless wiretaps and the intrusions of his special investigative unit—the ironically titled 'plumbers'—into the offices of Ellsberg's former psychoanalyst (Ellsberg, 2002). If nothing else, such extralegal efforts to smear whistleblowers into silence, suggest the rhetorical importance to information activists everywhere of a perception of probity and of a capital of trust.

Almost forty years on, the state partners with financiers and private infrastructure providers to try to muzzle WikiLeaks (Benkler, 2011). Besieged, Assange releases a US counterintelligence report from 2008 that identifies WikiLeaks' protection of source anonymity as the form of trust comprising its "center of gravity" (Horvath, 2008). This trust was famously compromised in the case of Chelsea Manning, of course, by human rather than technical factors. Manning confided in ex-hacker Adrian Lamo, who promptly betrayed this confidence by leaking to U.S. federal authorities and to the press.[4]

---

[4] See, for example, Fowler (2011); Gibney in O'Hehir (2013); Greenberg (2012); Leigh and Harding (2011).

But if WikiLeaks is enabled by the trust placed in its capacity to preserve source anonymity, anonymity's structural pair, publicity – in the form of highly visible, mediatized performances of personae – is equally critical to digital leaking's ecologies. In this regard, biographical inquiry works critically to determine what Assange and Snowden will stand for or represent. Plainly, both figures have, on occasion, urged the media to attend to their revelations and not to 'play the man'. However, the very lamenting by Assange and Snowden of *ad hominem* attacks folds into their public storying: it comprises one more step in their related but contrastive performances of the persona of the digital information activist.

Assange and Snowden: Two performances of persona

Filmed talking to Mark Davis for the latter's *Whistleblower* documentary while being made up to appear on Swedish television, Assange explains that WikiLeaks "needs a face" (Davis, 2010a). Back then, Sweden was friendly legal and promotional ground for Assange. Davis notes in voiceover that Assange is "stepping forward to promote the Iraq video" (Davis, 2010a). The video in question is WikiLeaks' edit of a U.S. Apache gunship recording tendentiously titled *Collateral Murder*. Arguably, its release on 5 April 2010 marked the point at which WikiLeaks went viral and Assange became an object of global controversy. "The public demands" explains Assange, "that WikiLeaks has a face. And actually [...] I'd prefer it if it didn't have a face ... [but] people just started inventing faces" (Davis, 2010a). With growing exposure, Assange concedes, albeit reluctantly, that WikiLeaks needs a character: an ethos, a speaking position, a mask or persona. To act as a mouthpiece, WikiLeaks needs a face (Munro, 2015).

But something in Assange's reluctance here fails to ring true. The fact is, we struggle as viewers to bracket out subsequent developments, in which Assange embraced a kind of rock star fame and moved to conflate his person with the project of WikiLeaks. Feigned or not, this perception of a false note goes to an ethopoetical point, namely that biography is a process of character construction whose frame of reference is the totality of an individual's dealings over time in the world. Within this frame of reference, biography makes its partisan choices, taking up and animating an individual's actions selectively. As metadata are selected to establish an individual's pattern of life, so are a person's actions chosen and reframed biographically. This reframing or uptake is a matter of *kairos*: it responds to partisan imperatives and situational opportunities.[5]

This is evidenced in the uses to which an interview with Assange is put. In another of Davis' documentaries, *Inside WikiLeaks*, a contented if somewhat smug Assange remarks that he is "untouchable now in this country". "Untouchable?" muses Davis, "that's a bit of hubris!" (Davis, 2010b). Alex Gibney (2013) uses this segment as stock footage in *We Steal Secrets: The Story of WikiLeaks*. However, Gibney elides the context of Assange's comments—a discussion of media coverage of the Afghan War Logs release—to segue from the hubris remark to the allegations of sexual assault. Plainly, Gibney's cut is tendentious, but it is Assange's self-presentation, promotion, and actions over time that imbue this linking with narrative and characterological plausibility. Indeed, stories of hubristic missteps start to cloud his performance as a digital information activist. Hubris in respect of the sex assault allegations, for example, when Assange invokes the prospect of rendition and conflates WikiLeaks with his private and legal personae to reframe a sex offense case as one concerning freedom of speech. Hubris, too, from the radical transparency advocate, who reacts furiously to *The Guardian*'s publication of details of his case, who attempts to gag colleagues and collaborators, and who tries to commoditize the information for which he claims to be the conduit (Ball, 2013). Hubris, also, in relation to redaction, where an infamous ambivalence to harm minimization invites the blunt but rhetorically effective 'blood on his hands' critique (Munro, 2015).

In July 2013, Snowden watched his surveillance revelations circulate globally just as his own movements ground to a halt. His onward travel stymied by the Obama administration's revocation of his passport, Snowden issued a statement explaining that the NSA's flagrant infringement of the Constitution had motivated his whistleblowing activities. Thanking friends "new and old, family and others", he noted that he remained "unbowed in his convictions and impressed at the efforts taken by so many" (Snowden, 2013a). Snowden's statement was issued by WikiLeaks. Indeed, it bears the hallmarks of Assange in messianic manifesto mode. Unquestionably, WikiLeaks was instrumental in Snowden's reaching Russia: off the front page and holed up in Ecuador's London embassy, Assange was quick to claim credit for orchestrating Snowden's flight.

Despite these interrelations, Snowden is hardly a mouthpiece for Assange. Plainly, comparisons between these two figures are numerous, and could be developed at length. For our purposes and in the interests of brevity, however,

---

[5] On *kairos*, see Sipiora and Baumlin (2002).

let us quickly contrast their respective parameters on and performances of the persona of the digital information activist. Compared with Assange, Snowden to date has been comparatively successful in containing his fame, constraining the ambit of his interventions and the nature of his impact. This is due partly to the nature of his material and the timing of its release, and partly to the management of the impression of the man.

The material: unlike WikiLeaks' earlier releases, Snowden's trove of data is able to be read as a coherent object: stolen from a single source, it is readily framed as so many indices of state mass surveillance regimes, so much proof of governmental overreach. This ease of legibility or relative agreement as to what the data stand for or represent, is evidenced by the way in which Snowden's revelations are widely credited, by supporters and detractors alike, with catalyzing current debates around surveillance and the national security state. Developments like the ruling in ACLU vs Clapper (07/05/2015), and the passage of the USA Freedom Act (02/06/2015), can be taken up as a legacy, or indeed vindication, of Snowden's acts.

The man: Snowden self-presents as a whistleblower, despite being precluded by the statute under which he is charged, the *Espionage Act of 1917*, from legally mounting a public interest defense. In interviews, teleconferenced speaker events and biopics, Snowden insistently frames himself as a conservative, Constitution-upholding libertarian, a patriot who has no truck with radical transparency, and who baulks not at state surveillance, but rather at governmental overreach. The biographical mode here is critical to Snowden's performance of the persona of the digital information activist.

Despite failing to join the elite Special Forces, as a patriot, he had tried to enlist; from a family of federal government employees, he has a longtime girlfriend to whom no serious mud will stick. With his undercover training and technical expertise established, Snowden cites watershed moments— outrage at national intelligence directors baldly and repeatedly lying to congressional committees — to trace a whistleblowing trajectory: stricken by conscience, with official channels unresponsive, an ordinary, albeit privileged guy with a comfortable life in Hawaii resorts to civil disobedience.[6]

It is here that Snowden's performance diverges most: his framing as a whistleblower is cleaner than that of Assange, who occupies multiple, overlapping offices. Likewise, Snowden's dealings with the press have tended to be less messy. In contradistinction to Assange, Snowden's public

---

[6] See, for example, Greenwald (2014); Snowden (2013b; 2013c).

prosecution of his case has turned on a largely collaborative, non-conflictive and non-confrontational relation to the fourth estate. An astute choice of media collaborators and a decidedly custodial, non-proprietary relation to the data have been paramount here, both to counter the 'Chinese agent' and 'Russian patsy' allegations, and to frame whistleblowing as the targeted, responsible leaking of secrets to expert journalists with a view to serving the public interest.

The Celebrity Digital Information Activist

Laura Poitras' *Citizenfour* (2014) is useful here: it effectively frames the persona of the celebrity digital information activist as emergent from a collaborative and mediatized ecology. In the documentary's final scenes, Snowden sits in a room somewhere in Moscow with his collaborator and advocate, seasoned journalist and former constitutional lawyer, Glenn Greenwald. Animated, Greenwald bears news for a weary but unbroken Snowden: another whistleblower is coming forward, some huge revelations about U.S. drone activities are on the horizon, along with concomitant risks. Presuming the place to be bugged, Greenwald doles out his news on paper, punctuating talk with dramatic pauses to scribble down details and to pass notes on. "That's actually … that's really dangerous on the source's side!" interjects Snowden, "Do they know how to take care of themselves? Do you know anything about them?"

It is a poignant moment in the film that acts as a reflexive rallying point. Earlier, Snowden had channeled Assange to expound on the hydra-headed, unstoppable nature of digital leaking: the state can silence an individual, but with governmental accountability absent and state overreach unchecked, others will be inspired to risk all and to leak. To be continued, the scene seems to announce. But this ending is more than portentous: it points to the partial nature of representation and the partisan work of the documentary genre. In addition, it stages leaking as a process of mediated uptakes in which information is received, translated and transformed. The camera lingers on Greenwald's hands: the hands of a Hermes figure, the trickster god of boundaries and of translators, patron of orators, player with fire, protector of thieves (Brown 1990; Serres 1982). The camera lingers as Greenwald writes, his jottings a performance of the paranoid spy thematics founding digital leaking's practices and mythologies.

Citizenfour ends with a tightly cropped pair of hands shredding Greenwald's notes. The tatters fall on a transparent tabletop and are later scooped up and removed. Behind these scribblings, we are drawn to conclude, sits another tale of data scraped and shifted, and pervading the scene, an intimation of another performance —a further inflection or translation— of the *persona* of the celebrity digital information activist.[7]

References

Assange, J., Appelbaum, J., Müller-Maguhn, A., & Zimmerman, J. (2012). *Cypherpunks Freedom and the Future of the Internet*. New York London: O/R Books.

Assange, J., & O'Hagan, A. (2013). *Julian Assange The Unauthorised Autobiography*. Edinburgh: Canongate Books.

Benkler, Y. (2011). A Free Irresponsible Press: WikiLeaks and the Battle over the Soul of the Networked Fourth Estate. *Harvard Civil Rights – Civil Liberties Law Review, 46*(2), 311-397.

Brevini, B., Hintz, A., & McCurdy, P. (Eds.). (2013). *Beyond WikiLeaks: Implications for the Future of Communications, Journalism and Society*. Basingstoke: Palgrave Macmillan.

Condon, B. (Director). (2013). *The Fifth Estate*. [Motion Picture]. United States: Dreamworks SKG.

Davis, M. (2010a). *The Whistleblower*. [Television broadcast]. Australia: SBS Dateline. http://www.sbs.com.au/news/dateline/story/whistleblower

Davis, M. (2010b). *Inside WikiLeaks*. [Television broadcast]. Australia: SBS Dateline. http://www.sbs.com.au/news/dateline/story/inside-wikileaks

Domscheit-Berg, D. (2011). *Inside WikiLeaks: My Time with Julian Assange at the World's Most Dangerous Website*. Victoria, Australia: Scribe Publications.

D'Orazio, V. (2014). *Beyond: Edward Snowden*. [E-comic]. Stormfront Entertainment.

Dreyfus, S. (2001). *Underground: Hacking, Madness and Obsession on the Electronic Frontier*. Australia: Random House.

Driessens, O. (2015). On the Epistemology and Operationalisation of Celebrity. *Celebrity Studies 6*(3), 370-373.

Ellsberg, D. (2002). *Secrets A Memoir of Vietnam and the Pentagon Papers*. United States: Penguin Books.

Fowler, A. (2011). *The Most Dangerous Man in the World*. United States: Skyhorse Publishing.

Fowler, E. (2003). *Literary Character: The Human Figure in Early English Writing*. Ithaca: Cornell University Press.

Frow, J. (2006). *Genre*. London and New York: Routledge.

---

[7] For an account of the editing deliberations in relation to this footage, see Packer (2014).

Gibney, A. (Director). (2013). *We Steal Secrets: The Story of WikiLeaks*. [Motion Picture]. United States: Universal Pictures.

Greenberg, A. (2012). *This Machine Kills Secrets: How WikiLeaks, Cypherpunks, and Hacktivists Aim to Free the World's Information*. United Kingdom: Virgin Books.

Greenwald, G. (2014). *No Place to Hide: Edward Snowden, the NSA and the Surveillance State*. London: Penguin Books.

Hacking, I. (1995). The Looping Effects of Human Kinds. In D. Sperber, D. Premack and A. James Premack (Eds.), *Causal Cognition A Multidisciplinary Debate* (pp. 351-383). Oxford, England: Clarendon Press.

Hacking, I. (2001). Inaugural Lecture: Chair of Philosophy and History of Scientific Concepts at the Collège de France, 16 January 2001. *Economy and Society 31*(1), 1-14.

Harding, L. (2014). *The Snowden Files The Inside Story of the World's Most Wanted Man*. United States: Vintage Books.

Horvath, M. (2008). U.S. Army Counterintelligence Ctr., Wikileaks.org—An Online Reference to Foreign Intelligence Services, Insurgents, or Terrorist Groups? (Mar. 18, 2008). Available at http://www.scribd.com/doc/28385794/Us-Intel-Wikileaks

Leigh, D., & Harding, L. (2011). *WikiLeaks: Inside Julian Assange's War on Secrecy*. Great Britain: Guardian Books.

Lucas, E. (2014). *The Snowden Operation: Inside the West's Greatest Intelligence Disaster*. [E-book]. United States: Amazon Digital Services.

Marshall, D. (2014). Persona Studies: Mapping the Proliferation of the Public Self. *Journalism 15*(2), 153-170.

Marshall, D., Moore, C. & Barbour, K. (2015). Persona as Method: Exploring Celebrity and the Public Self through Persona Studies. *Celebrity Studies 6*(3), 288-305.

Miller, C. (2001) Writing in a Culture of Simulation: Ethos Online. In P. Coppock (Ed.), *The Semiotics of Writing: Transdisciplinary Perspectives on the Technology of Writing* (pp. 253-297). Turnhout, Belgium: Brepols.

Munro, A. (2015). Assange and WikiLeaks: Secrets, Personae, and the Ethopoetics of Digital Leaking. *Persona Studies 1*(1).

Poitras, L. (Director). (2014). *Citizenfour*. [Motion Picture]. Radius-TWC.

Rall, T. (2015) *Snowden*. United States: Seven Stories Press.

Snowden, E. (2013a). 'Statement from Edward Snowden in Moscow'. https://wikileaks.org/Statement-from-Edward-Snowden-in.html Retrieved 10 Oct 2015.

Snowden, E. (2013b). *NSA Whistleblower Edward Snowden: 'I don't want to live in a society that does these sort of things' - video*. G. Greenwald. [Video Interview] United States: The Guardian US http://www.theguardian.com/world/video/2013/jun/09/nsa-whistleblower-edward-snowden-interview-video Retrieved 10 Oct 2015.

Snowden, E. (2013c). *Edward Snowden: 'The US government will say I aided our enemies' – video G. Greenwald* [Video interview]-. United States: The Guardian US http://www.theguardian.com/world/video/2013/jul/08/edward-snowden-video-interview Retrieved 10 Oct 2015.

Star, A. (Ed.). (2011). *Open Secrets WikiLeaks, War and American Diplomacy*. New York, NYC: The New York Times.

Woo, B., Rennie, J., & Poyntz, S. (2015). Scene Thinking. *Cultural Studies 29*(3), 285-297.

Corporate Colonization and the Myth of Authentic Journalism

William Huddy

Abstract. The notion of authentic journalism was put forth in a 2012 research report which suggests that the true authentic modern journalist must reject the pressures society imposes on them, including corporate persuasion. Authenticity, it's argued, is nested in existentialism, which posits journalists must reject the dehumanizing demands of conformism and refuse compromise of personal convictions that journalists confront. Herein lies the rub. When media conglomerates with well-intentioned goals of authentic bias-free reporting mixes with independent-thinking seasoned journalists, sometimes the pieces just don't fit together. That was the case with Brian Williams. When, after a ten year history of model job performance NBC decides that its credible news presenter fails to make the grade, it is the on-air face of Brian Williams that takes the hit. This critical review examines how Deetz's Critical Theory of Communication highlights a failure of not only Williams' journalistic ethos, but a failure of organizational culture (NBC Comcast-Universal) and the unseemly dismantling and embarrassment of one of its prized employees.

Keywords: Media, Journalism, Authenticity, Corporate Colonization

Introduction

"This guy is such a liar and everyone knows it." (Simeone, in Mahler, J., et al., N.Y. Times, Feb. 5, 2015)." "Only a pathetic creature would lie like that."(Continetti, Culture & Civilization, Mar., 2015)," "Lyin', Brian! (N.Y. Post. Feb 6, 2015)." These statements might reflect criticisms reserved for only the 'worst of humanity' and not someone who for a decade was considered the most trusted news and watched anchormen in American television journalism. But this is exactly the hellish drama that has dogged NBC News Anchor Brian Williams, who through a series of embellishments, exaggerations, and reported untruths, has remained sequestered, and out of the public eye since his last broadcast, February 7, 2015. Only recently (Sept. 25-28th, 2015) did Williams reappear in a reporting role covering the visit of Pope Francis on MSNBC.

After a successful career at sister network MSNBC, Williams' moment had come, when on December 2, 2004 he was named primary NBC Anchor replacing the retiring Tom Brokaw. For more than ten years (2004-2015), Williams led NBC News to the top of the heap in the news ratings race among major network news broadcasts (Bauder, 2014). "Brian is one of the most trusted journalists of our time," said NBC President Deborah Turness (Steinburg/Variety, 2014). Then, within 2 months of signing a reported 5 year/10-million dollars per year contract with NBC News and its parent corporation NBC/Universal, the bottom falls out for Brian Williams. Williams takes himself off the air.

A week later on February 10th, he's slapped with a six-month suspension of his duties as Managing Editor and NBC Nightly News Anchor, and the subject of widespread public condemnation and denunciation for his on-air actions involving, among other incidents, self-aggrandizing embellishments of his war coverage in Iraq during celebrity appearances on network talk shows. In the weeks and months that followed, "...almost none of his peers in the news business came to his support" (Steel, E., Somaiya, R., New York Times, 2015). The criticism of Williams was unrelenting, and it drew on other unrelated incidents:

His embellishment of his helicopter journey and questions about his other reporting undermined the trust viewers placed in him. In the six days since admitting his mistake, he was pilloried relentlessly online, with Twitter feeds mocking his character and amateur truth squads investigating his past reporting (Steel, 2015).

Following an imposed period of reflection, Williams could only explain later that his actions were a result of "ego." "Looking back, it had to have been ego that made me think I had to be sharper, funnier, quicker than anybody else (Williams, interview with Matt Lauer on "The Today Show," June 19, 2015)."

The job parameters of today's 21st century television news anchor requires much more than a pleasing smile, sweet demeanor, and above-average journalistic skills. Today's anchor must satisfy the above demands of a viewing public plus the imaginative manipulation of character imposed by a corporate colonization of character. Brian Williams' public crucifixion was not exclusively caused by his confessed "deep urge inside." Rather, his dilemma is the product of modern journalism meeting the corporate dragon, seeking shameless self-promotion, viewer ratings, and somehow, seeking and developing that ever elusive notion of authenticity, in a world lacking it.

The First Television Anchor

Thanks to Marybelle Lull of Cambridge, New York, who is reported to be the very first person to coin the term "anchor man" (Conway, 2014), attributed to the 20th century phenomenon of a news host and purveyor of news and information in the televised visual/oral format in the United States. The attribution by Lull was in reference to the television personality John Cameron Swayze (not regarded historically as a newsman, Swayze's work was that of a quiz show host), which then led to the very first reference to television news personality, Walter Cronkite, as "Anchorman" (p. 445). This tension among scholars starting in the 1950's brought forth the notion of "boundary work" within journalism, positing the question, what defines a television news anchor?

In 1964, Harold Wilensky argued that journalists were not professionals: "Since one does not need to earn a journalism educational degree or pass a test or certification process to become a journalist, the occupation appears too porous for *true professional status* (Wilensky, 1964, in Conway, p. 447)." Brian Williams never did earn his Bachelor's degree, dropping out of George Washington University to work as an intern in the Jimmy Carter administration. But shortly after that, in part based on his authoritative on-air presentation skills (honed at NBC affiliate KOAM-TV, Pittsburg, Kansas), Williams did ink multiple million-dollar contracts. Perhaps only after Williams became a multi-millionaire would Wilensky find a change of heart and label him a "true professional."

Celebrity Journalism, and the Lure of Big Money

Saturday Night Live Comedian Norm MacDonald may have had it right when he suggested in 1987 that NBC & CBS morning host Bryant Gumble's short lived retirement was driven by one thing; money. Macdonald told guests at a White House Correspondents Dinner that Gumble "…had a change of heart" in announcing his retirement. "Bryant, in his heart, is a newsman," quipped Macdonald. "And after a few weeks of retirement, he (Gumble) realized that he missed the excitement and thrill… that you can only get, by making millions and millions of dollars (Macdonald, 1987)." The comedian's cynicism proved prophetic, not just for the successful Gumble, but for others too, as salaries for news talent went through the roof.

The injection in the 1980's of multi-million dollar salaries for television news anchors (particularly at the medium to major market affiliate level) took news anchors from 'journeyman' journalist status, to 'celebrity' status, overnight. Advertising revenues supported by record numbers of television viewers created the lucrative and profitable market for paying big money for news 'talent', and this is the culture that led to Williams' meteoric rise.

In December of 2014, it was reported NBC Universal and Williams had agreed on a new 5-year, 10 million dollar per-year employment contract. In December, things looked very bright indeed for Brian Williams. NBC would continue its dominance in the television news ratings race, but how quickly things would change. By mid-February of the following year, Williams took himself off the air, and NBC News executives slapped a six month suspension on Williams' managing editor and on-air duties. At that time Williams acknowledged the news he was creating had become bigger than the news he was reporting.

A Search for Authenticity

It would be fair to assume that the "model" for the consummate television news anchor personality in 1952 included the descriptive communication variables of oral clarity, interpersonal trust (Knapp and Miller, 1985), warmth, reasonableness, and later on, good looks (a pleasing on-air presence). But there was another quality that anchors in television's infancy possessed that somehow was present in the day, but lost over time. That quality embraced by television personalities of the day was a combination of perhaps all of the above, plus that notion of the authentic personality.

Authenticity, it's argued, is nested in the notion of existentialism. But for the early existentialist thinkers of the day (Kierkegaard, Nietzsche and Heidegger) to think that such a highly regarded concept could be attached to a medium highlighted by artificiality and sensationalism was improbable and perhaps preposterous. But it was authenticity that seemed to be present in the "successful" television news programs of the day.

To television news executives seeking higher viewer ratings and complementary advertising revenues, not all good journalists possessed the sought-after qualities cited above. An even fewer number of those qualified journalists represented an essence of authenticity. Brian Williams may have been one who almost defined the 'total package.' But then again, perhaps after the corporate sponsored 'Brian Williams Inquiry,' Williams did not meet the personality traits defined by NBC; traits that might suggest not everyone is "cut out" to imbibe this treasured nexus called 'authenticity.' Media scholars such as Kristoffer Holt have argued:

> Kierkegaard tells the reader that his book is not meant for those whose critical and aesthetic education comes from reading newspapers, but for 'rational creatures' who have the 'time and patience to read a little book.' There is a dimension of media-criticism in existential thought that reacts against mediated sensationalism, shallowness, and 'idle talk' (Kierkegaard & Hannay, 2001, in Holt, 2012, p. 2).

Holt effectively argues that among journalism professionals in 1977, there was a "framework" of good practices to "avoid herd mentality" in the pursuit of a story, and to "embrace freedom and responsibility" when working to cite and report events of human successes and tragedies. A "moral guide", writes Holt, is omnipresent when the constraints and oppression of corporate systems bear down on individual freedom of thought when reporting the news. He argues that in the quest of seeking out that elusive 'authenticity' in a world framed by a desire for viewer ratings and shareholder profit, authenticity is in fact abandoned or misplaced and that all moral claims to authenticity as defined by existentialist thought is lost. Perhaps, as some would argue, authenticity (as defined), is nothing but an illusion in this current television news environment.

According to the reliable internet source (IMD – Internet Movie Database, in Continetti, 2015), Brian Williams appeared (as himself) on as many as 76 news, talk, entertainment, and variety radio and television shows. Presumably it was the corporate parent company, NBC Universal, and its subsidiary (NBC News) that booked and coordinated these appearances. A fair assumption was that corporate executives believed Williams, appearing as himself, would engage his hosts and audiences and thereby boost his credibility as an 'authentic' television news personality. What happened in reality was that over an extended period of time, either because of a memory-loss issue, or through a contrived self-destructive effort to boost his own self-worth through a series of exaggerations, his credibility declined and efforts to boost his authentic stature instead failed miserably.

Deetz: Guided under a Corporate Umbrella

Perhaps as Soren Kierkegaard believed that "both the news media and the bourgeois church-Christianity" were societal obstacles for the possibility of living authentically (Holt, p. 5) and also an institutional impediment to the freethinking man, Stanley Deetz within the Critical Theory of Communication believes that corporations in modernity control people's free destiny in much the same way. He argues:

> In many respects, the corporate sector has become the primary institution in modern society, overshadowing the state in controlling and directing of individual lives and influencing collective social development. Workplace values and practices extend into non-work life through time structuring, educational content, economic distributions, product development, and creation of needs (Deetz, 1992).

Deetz correctly highlighted 23 years ago the movement by corporations to control many aspects of our individual lives, including the media conglomerates (mega-corporations) or those 'in charge' of the fourth estate and the constitutional guarantees of a "free press":

> We would probably be greatly concerned if an institution like the church or state came to dominate the media, but such an eighteenth-century mindset fails to account for the actual institutional alignment today. How would people feel if the government or church produced a "commercial" (or propaganda, depending on the institution of concern) every ten to fifteen minutes on the television and had primary say over the programming? We know something of that, because we know moments in history when such domination was accepted *and* when it was rejected (Deetz, p. 31).

Deetz believes that the encroachment of modern corporate activities into "nonwork life" might properly be called a "colonizing" activity – a colonization of the life world (Habermas 1984/1987, in Deetz, 1992, p. 18). For 13 years, Comcast (the parent corporation) and NBC Universal relied on Brian Williams to act as its primary spokesman on the flagship NBC Nightly News. And just two months before suspending Williams, the parent corporation re-signed Williams to his largest contract ever. What happened to so radically change the direction of this multi-billion dollar corporation (141.5 billion dollar market capitalization as of this writing) and its support and reliance of this long-time employee, Brian Williams?

It would be fair to assume that the individual labors and activities of a television news anchor and managing editor (in this case Brian Williams) were almost completely controlled by its parent corporation. To suggest that Williams' repeated on-air embellishments (or perhaps better referred to as "personal titillations" or accounts) on late night entertainment shows were not encouraged or prompted by the corporate promotions department prior to the avalanche of criticism, would be disingenuous. NBC News, and its employee Brian Williams, may have pushed the envelope of authenticity and credibility too far.

What is unusual about the level of criticism, is that most of the vicious criticism was directed almost entirely at Brian Williams, with very little reserved for the parent corporation of NBC News, NBC/Comcast Universal Inc. But NBC News was not without suspicion.

In the four years since the Philadelphia, PA-based cable giant Comcast took over NBC Universal, corporate executives (including 47-year old News Director Deborah Turness) had been under the gun putting out fires throughout their news department: Anchor/Reporter Ann Curry left the company under a cloud of bad feelings when she was removed from her role with the *Today Show; Meet The Press* moderator David Gregory, in an awkward transition, was replaced by political reporter Chuck Todd; and newly appointed Executive Director Jamie Horowitz (ESPN) was replaced after only three months on the job after "...trying to fix the *Today Show* (Burrough, 2015)."

In 1992 Deetz warned of the dangers of unfettered corporate influence, influence not necessarily in the public interest, in the fast-paced consolidation of the mass media industry in the United States. Asking, "What happens when news programs have to show a profit (p. 32)," Deetz suggests when elements of corporate invasiveness are present in areas of story selection, editing, on-air presentation, and promotion. He asserts: "All information today, whether news, entertainment, or commercial, has to be considered as sponsored information". From appearances on late-night variety shows (Late Night with David Letterman, Saturday Night Live, The Daily Show w/ Jon Stewart, etc.) and the personal recollections and recounts of previous reporting assignments, to the on-air apologia offered by Williams on February 7, 2015; all of these events controlled and strategized by the corporation, not in the public interest, but rather recognizing the corporate responsibility and value to stakeholders of the corporation, also known as shareholders.

However, the Williams on-air apology may not have been the smoothest of choreographed actions by the network, but perhaps just one which 'scooted-by' the heavy-handed network puppeteering. An account published by the magazine Vanity Fair (April 30, 2015) reflects a panicked and out-of-control corporate head office when word of a Williams-inked apology was about to be broadcast nationwide.

Turness was still trying to grasp the gravity of the situation when the *Stars and Stripes* article (revealing Williams' embellishments) went online. At that point her biggest concern was the apology Williams was preparing to read to viewers on his broadcast that evening. He was already taping segments as he and Turness began swapping e-mails on its all-important wording. Turness and the other executives who had gotten involved quickly became frustrated, as they would remain for days, with Williams's inability to explain himself (Burroughs, 2015)." "We got the best [apology] we could," said one NBC insider.

Perhaps the Brian Williams on-air apology of February 7th was the closest viewers of the NBC Nightly News will ever get to the 'unfettered truth' of what happened, a truth by an authentic journalist not vetted in its entirety by the corporate parent, Comcast/NBC Universal.

Conclusion

As consumers of public information, we are under no illusion that the consuming public has all the information to make a precise assessment into the inner-workings of a private corporation. In fact, the public is not privy to the very private negotiations and life of Brian Williams, and few know the specific reasons for this very public dismissal and embarrassment. What the public is aware of is that 1) Williams was involved in several, if not many instances, of inaccurate accounts and embellishment (lying) of facts involving his reporting of major news events, and 2) The uncertainties in the public domain include the reasons why this unfolded in the manner it did. Whether these embellishments were driven by a personality/character flaw (in spite of being a respected and a well-liked 22-year NBC employee), or whether he was prompted, encouraged, or directed by corporate officials to portray himself, not in the public's interest, but in an embellished light in search of audience ratings and corporate shareholder value, remains to be known.

References

Baker, K. C. (2015, February 23). *Under Fire*. People, 83 (3), 63-64.

Bradshaw, K. A., Foust, J. C., & Bernt, J. (2005). Local Television News Anchor's Public Appearances. *Journal of Broadcasting and Electronic Media.* 49 (2). 166-181.

Burrough, B. (2015, April 30). The Inside Story of the Civil War For the Soul of NBC News. *Vanity Fair.* Retrieved January 25, 2016
http://www.vanityfair.com/news/2015/04/nbc-news-brian-williams-scandal-comcast.

Continetti, M. (2015, March). The Dishonor of Brian Williams. *Commentary.* 139 (3). 55-56.

Conway, M. (2014). The origins of television's "anchor man": Cronkite, Swayze, and journalism boundary work. *American Journalism.* 31 (4), 445-461.

Deetz, S. (2003). Corporate Governance, Communication, and Getting Social Values into the Decisional Chain. *Management Communication Quarterly.* 16 (4). 606-611.

Deetz, S. (1997). The Contribution of Communication Studies to the Emerging Age of Negotiation. *Florida Communication Journal.* 25 (1). 11-23.

Deetz, S. (1993). Corporations, The Media Industry, and Society: Ethical Imperatives and Responsibilities. *Paper Presented at the 43rd Annual Meeting of the International Communication Association. May 27-31, 1993. Washington D.C.*

Deetz, S. (1992). *Democracy in an Age of Corporate Colonization.* State University of New York Press. Albany, N.Y.

Deetz, S. (1990). Reclaiming the Subject Matter as a Guide to Mutual Understanding: Effectiveness and Ethics in Interpersonal Interaction. *Communication Quarterly.* 38 (3). Pgs. 226-243.

Deetz, S. (1987). Stories, Accounts, and Organizational Power. *American Communication Association Bulletin.* 61. 36-41.

Gilmour, D. A., & Quanbeck, A. (2010). Hegemony: Quiet Control Over

Convergence Textbook Content. *The Review of Communication.* 10 (4). 324-341.

Holt, K. (2012). Authentic Journalism? A Critical Discussion About Existential Authenticity in Journalism Ethics. *Journal of Mass Media Ethics.* 27. 2-14

Knapp, M., & Miller, G. (1985). *Handbook of Interpersonal Communication.* Newbury Park, CA. Sage.

Kurtz, H. (2012). *Walter Cronkite Would Be Fired Today.* Newsweek. 155. 22. May 28, 2012.

Mazer, J. (2013). From Apologia to Farewell: Dan Rather, CBS News, and Image Restoration Following the 60 Minutes "Memogate" Scandal. *Ohio Communication Journal.* 51. 168-181.

MacDonald, N (1987). *The White House Correspondents Dinner.* Retrieved from: https://youtu.be/d5kpXhq5nHM.

N.Y. Post (2015) *Lyin' Brian.* Cover Photo. Feb. 6, 2015.

Simeone, C., in Mahler, J., Somaiya, R., Steel, E. (2015, February 5) With an Apology, Brian Williams Digs Himself in Deeper in Copter Tale. *NY Times.* p. A1.

Steel, E., & Somaiya, R. (2015). *Brian Williams Suspended From NBC for 6 Months Without Pay.* Retrieved December 15, 2014, from International New York Times: http://www.nytimes.com/2015/02/11/business/media/brian-williams-suspendedby-nbc-news-for-six-months.html?_r=0.

Steinberg, B. (2014, December 15). *Brian Williams Renews Contract with NBC News.* Variety. http://variety.com/2014/tv/news/brian-williams-renews-contract- with-nbc-news-1201379585/.

Williams, B. (2015). Interview with Matt Lauer on the Today Show. http:/ney.cnn.com/2015/06/19/media/brian-williams-nbc-speaks-on-today-show/

Witkin, C. (2014, November 10). ABC News Anchor David Muir: The New Star of Network News. *People.* 94-95.

Celebrity Culture and the Canadian Broadcasting Corporation: Jian Ghomeshi, Global Others, and Sexual Violence

Kiera Obbard

Abstract. With Jian Ghomeshi's recent sexual abuse scandal dominating Canadian media headlines throughout the past year, nationalist rhetoric of Canada as a nation of peace and gender equality has come into question. This paper uses Jian Ghomeshi as a case study to explore the construction of state celebrities by the Canadian Broadcasting Corporation and the state celebrity's role in the nation-building project. By analyzing the media's use of rape myths and rhetoric of sexually deviant Others, and by exploring how the media continue to represent Ghomeshi's persona in relation to the nation-building project, this paper explores the ways in which Canadian media reinvigorates nationalist discourse while remaining complicit in a culture of violence against women in Canada.

Keywords: Jian Ghomeshi, Canadian Broadcasting Corporation, state celebrity, sexual assault, nationalism

Introduction

Recently, the Canadian media landscape has been littered with stories of sexual violence, directly challenging the long-standing national discourse of Canada as a progressive, tolerant nation. With cases like Jian Ghomeshi dominating headlines in the past year, the state of equality, celebrity, and journalism in Canada have been heavily criticized. As Canadian media construct a narrative of a sexually violent celebrity culture within the Canadian Broadcasting Corporation (CBC)—drawing on long-used discourses of global 'Others' to reinforce their representational strategy—these narratives offer a site from which to critique Canadian nationalism, the production of celebrity, and the perpetuation of normative scripts of sexual violence in Canada.

Since the story first broke on October 26, 2014, media coverage of Ghomeshi has focused on the inherent monstrousness of Ghomeshi's character, sensationalizing and strategically narrating the story to the public both in Canada and abroad. Drawing from their position as neutral third-party reporter, Canadian media (including the CBC and private media outlets) portray themselves as providing value-free information to the public, and yet their representational strategies point towards an unquestioned power hierarchy and an unacknowledged role in the creation of this toxic celebrity culture. Using Jian Ghomeshi's recent sexual abuse scandal as a case study, this paper interrogates the construction of the state celebrity by the CBC. Through close analysis of the media coverage of Ghomeshi's fallen celebrity status, this paper explores the problematic gendered, racialized ways in which Canadian media texts both situate the narrative of Ghomeshi's fall from Canadian fame and continue to use his fallen persona to resituate and reinvigorate nationalist discourse, all-the-while remaining complicit in a culture of violence against women in Canada.

Jian Ghomeshi

On Sunday, October 26, 2014, the CBC announced that it was severing ties with Ghomeshi, co-creator and host of CBC Radio One's highly successful show *Q*, because of information they had obtained about the star, as executive vice-president Heather Conway described in an internal CBC memo. A few hours later, Ghomeshi's lawyers had launched a CAD $55 million lawsuit against the CBC alleging breach of confidence, bad faith and defamation. Fearing public exposure by freelance journalist Jesse Brown and the Toronto Star's Kevin Donovan, who had been approached by women alleging abuse by Ghomeshi and had been working on the story for months, Ghomeshi attempted to pre-emptively code his termination as the vindictive allegations of a "jilted ex-girlfriend and freelance writer". Ghomeshi posted an explanation of his termination to Facebook, stating: "I've been fired from the CBC because of the risk of my private sex life being made public...The implication may be made that this [sexual activity] happens non-consensually. And that will be a lie" (Donovan and Brown, 2014; *Full Text*). Within days, however, multiple women came forward alleging varying forms of abuse, and on Wednesday, November 26, 2014, Ghomeshi surrendered to Toronto Police and was charged with four counts of sexual assault and one count of overcoming resistance by choking. Meanwhile, an independent investigation into CBC's handling of Ghomeshi was launched and, as more women and a male former York University student came forward with allegations of sexual assault, more charges were laid (Donovan and Hasham, 2014). After the independent review conducted by Janice Rubin was released to the public in April 2015, the CBC severed ties with former head of radio Chris Boyce and human resources director Todd Spencer for their 'mishandling' of employee complaints made against Ghomeshi (*CBC Inquiry*). Recently, crown prosecutors dropped two of the seven sexual assault charges laid against Ghomeshi. Two separate trial dates have been set for February and June of 2016 (Willms, 2015).

The State Celebrity

To begin our discussion of Ghomeshi's rise to and fall from celebrity status in Canada, we must first situate his celebrity in relation to the state. In "Theorizing the state celebrity: a case study of the Canadian Broadcasting Corporation," authors Cormack and Cosgrave (2014) argue that celebrity should be analyzed in relation to the state as broadcaster because celebrity functions differently in relation to the state. Using prominent CBC celebrities as case studies, the authors establish a framework for analyzing the state celebrity as produced by state broadcasting systems for the purpose of promoting and protecting national identity, supporting state formation, and legitimating state values and cultural policies. The celebrity in this context is an agent of the state whose carefully constructed persona functions simultaneously as a pedagogical and a promotional tool, both demonstrating and reinforcing national identity to a national and global audience. State celebrities in this context not only help to create and enforce national identity, but "work to celebrate the state in all its manifestations—technologies, personnel, policies, practices, and ideologies" (Cormack and Cosgrave, 2014, p. 335). Similarly to P. Marshall's (2010) definition of the celebrity which, he argues, "has been and is increasingly a pedagogical tool and specifically a pedagogical aid in the discourse of the self", the state celebrity functions as a pedagogical tool of the state and aids in the discourse of the state, instructing the public on what constitutes proper Canadian values and what it means to be Canadian (p. 36).

The CBC as a state broadcaster and creator of state celebrities is particularly interesting because of Canada's complicated history with and anxiety over Canadian cultural content (CanCon). With the Broadcasting Act (1991), the CBC was mandated as the national public broadcaster to "provide radio and television services...that informs, enlightens, and entertains" Canadians. The CBC's programming is required to "be predominantly and distinctively Canadian," to "contribute to the flow and exchange of cultural expression," to "reflect the multicultural and multiracial nature of Canada," and to "contribute to shared national consciousness and identity," to name a few (Broadcasting Act [S.C. 1991, c. 11]). The CBC's responsibility to CanCon and to creating a shared national identity are significant in analyzing state celebrities and, in particular, Ghomeshi's celebrity persona. Faced with a long crisis of Canadian identity—an anxiety over being subsumed by the American cultural 'Other' and an inability to create a cohesive narrative out of multiple cultural and regional differences—the CBC constructs state celebrities for the purpose of entertaining, enlightening, and, importantly, informing Canadians on what it means to be Canadian (Keohane, 1997). In practice, this educating of Canadians serves as a means of protecting and defending Canadian values from global 'Others' who threaten our shared national identity.

Typical of nation-building projects, which depict 'acceptable' types of masculinity in relation to the state, the CBC operates with a number of prominent (predominantly white) male celebrities who play out types of masculinity as representatives of the state (Cormack and Cosgrave, 2014). In their study, Cormack and Cosgrave (2014) discuss how celebrities Don Cherry, Rick Mercer, Peter Mansbridge, and George Stroumboloupolous perform varying types of masculinity in their representations of the state – the aggressive, pro-military state; the state as humorous, friendly protector; the pedagogical state as representation of truth; and the state as host to all things Canadian, respectively. In a similar manner, Ghomeshi performs a specific type of masculinity in his role as representative of the state.

Ghomeshi was born in London, England in 1967 to Iranian parents Farhang (Frank) and Azar (Sara) Ghomeshi, and his family immigrated to Canada when he was seven years old. In his recent memoir entitled *1982,* and in multiple articles published since his rise to fame, Ghomeshi discusses his long-felt anxiety over his Iranian heritage, remarking on the profound impact the 1979 Iranian revolution had on his sense of national identity (Ghomeshi 2012). In an article written for the Pittsburgh Post-Gazette, Ghomeshi states of his Iranian heritage and the revolution: "'I was too young to have the tools to understand the political realities of what was going on, and certainly not to understand stereotyping. All I knew was that we came from this evil place'" (Roth, 2014). Ghomeshi continues, telling Roth that he "loves the way Toronto has become the polyglot city of scores of ethnic groups," and that his one worry for fellow Iranian-Canadians is that they will fail to integrate into Canadian culture on an economic, social, and political level (Roth, 2014). Ghomeshi's complicated relationship with his heritage, including his admission that his family was secularist, positions him in an ideal cultural location as a representative of the state, and his narrative of integration into Canada positions Ghomeshi as an ideal to which immigrant Canadians should aspire. Additionally, while attending York University, Ghomeshi minored in Women's Studies and advocated for women's rights as President of the Council of the York Federation of Students, positioning him in line with nationalist discourse of gender equality in Canada. Ghomeshi's star quality and his experience as a member of Moxy Früvous, a politically satirical folk-pop band, made him appealing to a younger audience. For the CBC, then, Ghomeshi represented a younger, multi-cultural audience that had successfully integrated into Canadian society and that was receptive to, and cared about, women's issues. Faced with years of ratings in decline, anxieties over CanCon, and an inability to reach a younger audience both at home and abroad, Ghomeshi became an integral component to the rejuvenation of the CBC. As the National Post reflects, the positioning of Ghomeshi's persona was so successful that "By the time he moved into the 10a.m. slot...the deal was sealed, and *Q* became the ticket to Canadian exposure for everyone from new artists to global celebrities, breaking ground for the CBC in U.S. markets" (Brean, 2014). With his importance at both a national and a global level established, Ghomeshi became not simply a representation of a multicultural, liberal, feminist-friendly Canada, but he became a cultural icon, a means through which Canadians new and old learned what constitutes proper Canadian values.

Deviant Sexuality and the Monstrous Other

If Ghomeshi as cultural icon served to teach us about Canada as a multicultural, tolerant, equal-opportunity nation, the media discourse of Ghomeshi following his fall from grace similarly serves as a pedagogical tool—one that aids in the discourse of the nation by positioning Ghomeshi as a sexually deviant, racialized Other. In her recent book, Samita Nandy (2015) discusses Ghomeshi's rise and fall in Canadian culture. Drawing on Sharif Khan's discussion of Russell Williams' fall from fame, Nandy (2015) notes that before charges were laid, "Ghomeshi was represented as a Toronto-based public radio star who showcased Canada's cultural difference in comparison to America's scandal-driven Hollywood...Following Ghomeshi's sexual abuse scandals, however, he became the walking embodiment of sociopathic behavior and anti-heroism" (p. 192). More than becoming an anti-hero, media constructions of Ghomeshi's 'sexual abuse scandals' position him as monstrous in relation to his racially constructed sexual deviance and deviation from Canada's moral consciousness.

In media coverage of the case since the story initially broke out, many journalists have claimed shock and disgust over the apparent 'hidden monstrousness' of Ghomeshi's personality. Canadian news outlets such as Maclean's state that "If there was a collective shock [in Canada], it wasn't based on the Jian we didn't know, the Mr. Hyde we never saw. It was based on the Jian many had known for decades—the Jian hiding in plain sight" (Kingston, 2014). The Waterloo Region Record asks, "Is it possible that the most beloved broadcaster in Canada—which is what he was—is actually a sick sexual monster?" (Rubinoff, 2014). Additionally, we are told that as Canadians, we don't like "that we let the monster into our homes" (Wynne-Jones, 2014). This representational strategy of positioning the rapist-as-monster is not uncommon in media reports of rape and sexual assault. Many studies have been conducted analyzing the perpetuation of rape myths in media coverage of sexual assault—coverage which frequently positions rapists using monster imagery and survivors using imagery of either the virgin (read: acceptable, believable victim) or the whore (read: a promiscuous woman who 'asked for it') (O'Hara, 2012; Barnett, 2008; Mason and Monckton-Smith, 2008; Soothill et al., 1990). This discourse is harmful, not only because we know it to be untrue—many studies show that sexual offenders are much the same as other people and the majority of women are assaulted by someone they know—but also because it positions rapists not as everyday people who commit violent assaults against others, but as unintelligible, unknowable monsters (read: non-human beings) (W. Marshall, 1996; Stermac et. al., 1995). The framing of the rapist-as-monster makes it increasingly difficult for the public to identify and accept that beloved celebrities, with whom we develop para-social relationships, are capable of committing rape, leading to increases in victim-blaming and a tendency to discredit and disbelieve those who come forward with allegations of sexual assault. In addition, the discourse that frames rapists as monsters positions rapists as existing outside of the narrative of the nation and allows for the Othering of other nations to occur. There is no place for rapists or sexual assault within the discourse of the tolerant, progressive, and equality-touting nation, and therefore when rape does occur, according to this narrative, it must be attributed to the inherent monstrousness of the rapist—and not, importantly, to any societal structures of inequality or misogyny within Canada. Our nationalist discourse teaches us that Canada is a nation free from violence, poverty, discrimination, and more, and it positions Canada largely in terms of what it is not—in other words, a nation where sexual assault occurs. This very gendered, sexualized, and racialized nationalist rhetoric relies in part upon media representation of sexual assault as a crime that exists in other countries—particularly, in recent years, in countries such as India, Afghanistan, and Iraq. Questions about gender and sexuality taken up by this nationalist discourse, such as "where does rape occur?" work to promote the conception of gender equality in Canada without the state ever having to actually work towards achieving it. The role of the media in relation to this Othering is significant. By sensationalizing headlines of rapes in other predominantly non-developed countries, and by referring to these countries as barbaric or savage because rapes occur there, the media contributes to the nationalist discourse and, ultimately, answers the question: rape happens 'over there'. More than just positioning rape as occurring only in 'Othered' places, the media's framing of Ghomeshi (and other rapists) as monster constructs a narrative of what kind of rape *does* occur in Canada, and what kind of *person* commits rape in Canada. In this understanding of the monstrous nature of the rapist, Canadian culture and larger societal structures of inequality remain uninterrogated and our focus remains solely on the hidden monstrousness of the person who rapes.

The representation of the rapist as a monster draws back to narratives from nineteenth and twentieth century Gothic fiction in which monsters were presented often as physically disfigured abhorrent figures, that represented repressed deviant sexuality and, importantly, threatened the purity of predominantly white women. In *Skin Shows: Gothic Horror and the Technology of Monsters,* Judith Halberstam (1995) argues that "Gothic fiction is a technology of subjectivity, one which produces the deviant subjectivities opposite which the normal, the healthy, and the pure can be known" (p. 2). Halberstam (1995) notes of the monster in particular that, as an economic form, it "condenses various racial and sexual threats to nation, capitalism, and the bourgeoisie in one body" (p. 3). Media depictions of Ghomeshi as monstrous and the correlations drawn between Ghomeshi and Mr. Hyde reinvigorate this nationalist fear of the sexually deviant 'Other,' tying Ghomeshi's behavior into a long history of rhetoric surrounding foreign bodies and deviant sexuality. In addition to depicting Ghomeshi as sexually deviant, this rhetoric positions Ghomeshi as standing opposite the 'normal, the healthy, and the pure' sexual activity of Canadians—he becomes, in other words, the mark of deviance against which proper Canadian sexuality is defined.

In many ways, the CBC's active framing of Ghomeshi as the rapist/monster also mirrors the narratives surrounding Muslim sexuality as simultaneously repressed and perverse, as the sexually deviant Other that threatens Canadian nationalism, which have become increasingly narrated through Western media outlets since the terrorist attacks on September 11, 2001 (Puar, 2007). This becomes even more evident in articles in Canadian media that draw linkages between the Ghomeshi scandal and the reported terrorist attack on Parliament Hill on October 22, 2014. Although there do not appear to be any news articles that attempt to directly tie Ghomeshi's deviant sexual behavior to his Muslim background, he is included in a few articles decrying Canada's loss of innocence in 2014. Interestingly, the CBC ran an article that draws a relationship between Ghomeshi and the Parliament Hill shootings of October 2014, noting of the latter that "The headline on American news website *The Daily Beast* proclaimed: 'Terrorist Ends Canada's Innocence.' (Semple, 2014). In this article, Jeff Semple notes that although both stories are different, they are told with a similar narrative: a betrayal of Canadian values and the loss of Canadian innocence. Thus, Ghomeshi's monstrosity lies not only in his sexually deviant behavior (sexual assault) but also in his betrayal of the nation and the CBC—a betrayal that must be rectified in order to protect the nationalist rhetoric of Canada. Ghomeshi's deviance from Canada's moral consciousness poses a significant threat to Canadian nationalism and the CBC's nation-building project because it points to the performativity inherent in his state persona. Ghomeshi's sexual deviancy creates fissures in the foundation of Canada as a nation of peace and gender equality, sheds light on the systemic sexual violence in existence at the CBC and in the broader Canadian media culture, and points to the fallibility of the nation-building project. The representational strategies of positioning Ghomeshi as monstrous 'Other,' then, serve to reinsert Ghomeshi into the nationalist discourse by positioning him as an evil against which all Canadians should define their moral consciousness.

Conclusion

Over the past few years, Western media has seen an increase in reporting on sexual assaults and, in Canada in particular, an increase in public engagement with and outrage over violence against women. In this political climate, and considering the racially, sexually fraught relationship Western countries have with Muslim identities since the War on Terror began[1], the framing of Ghomeshi as rapist/monster and sexually deviant 'Other' is significant. This reliance on harmful rape myths and narratives of Muslim sexuality obscures the many systems of oppression that enable sexual assault to occur in Canada. This emphasis on Ghomeshi's monstrousness and on the often sensationalized re-tellings of sexual assault at his hands works to further victimize women, turning their experiences of violence into a pornographic spectacle to be consumed and into a pedagogical tool from which the Canadian moral consciousness is reaffirmed (Smart, 2002). Rather than interrogating the complex cultural conditions, situation, and events that led to Ghomeshi's rise to fame and ability to use his influence to further victimize women, these narratives position Ghomeshi as simply existing outside of Canada's moral order. By presenting Ghomeshi as a monster, he comes to embody all that the 'proper Canadian' is not; he produces a disciplinary effect and, as a mark of deviance against which proper Canadian sexuality is defined, he teaches the Canadian public what constitutes normal sexual behavior. Even in his fall from fame, Ghomeshi's persona is reconstructed and repurposed to further the CBC's nation-building project.

---

[1] Recently in Canada, former Prime Minister Stephen Harper has been accused of promoting xenophobia and Islamophobia through his continued attacks on Muslim headware and his recent vow to create the 'barbaric cultural practices' hotline, a hotline which purports to "protect women and girls from forced marriage and other barbaric practices" (Barber, 2015).

These racialized narratives of the rapist-as-monster diminish the CBC's and other media outlets' accountability in creating this toxic celebrity culture. Instead of analyzing their role in creating this toxic celebrity culture in Canada, the (predominantly male) journalists use their positions of power[2] to re-work these stories into a cultural narrative about believable sexual assault and proper Canadian values. Through their framing of Ghomeshi and the women's experiences, our public and private broadcasters make the trauma these women endured into a pornographic spectacle, repurposing their trauma in order to portray Ghomeshi as a hidden monster lurking in their (morally conscious) midst (Smart, 2002; Heberle, 1996). Thus, the narratives of sexual assault in Canadian media remain uninterrogated, undisrupted, and depersonalized, and are used not to protect women from sexual violence or help women deal with trauma, but to frame Ghomeshi's sexual violence in such a way that it reinforces the nationalist discourse that his deviance threatened to undermine.

References

Barber, J. (2015, October 2). Canada's Conservatives vow to create 'barbaric cultural practices' hotline. *The Guardian,* Retrieved October 2, 2015, from http://www.theguardian.com/world/2015/oct/02/canada-conservatives-barbaric-cultural-practices-hotline.

Barnett, B. (2008). Framing Rape: An Examination of Public Relations Strategies in the Duke University Lacrosse Case. *Communication, Culture & Critique,* 179-202. Retrieved September 12, 2015, from http://libaccess.mcmaster.ca.libaccess.

lib.mcmaster.ca/login?url=http://search.ebscohost.com/login.aspx?direct=true&db=cms&AN=33377803&site=ehost-live&scope=site.

Brean, J. (2014, October 31). Jian Ghomeshi's journey: From immigrant's son to cultural icon to pariah. *National Post.* Retrieved March 8, 2015, from http://news.nationalpost.com/news/canada/jian-ghomeshis-journey-from-immigrants-son-to-cultural-icon-to-pariah.

Brown, J. (2015, May 5). Why some of Jian Ghomeshi's accusers don't want to 'tell all'. *The Guardian,* Retrieved May 20, 2015, from http://www.theguardian.com/commentisfree/2015/may/05/why-some-of-jian-ghomeshis-accusers-dont-want-to-tell-all.

---

[2] In May 2015, Jesse Brown wrote an article for the Guardian detailing how Kevin Donovan, the investigative reporter for the Toronto Star who helped break the story, is writing a 'tell-all' book about Ghomeshi's 'secret life' despite concerns from the women about being exposed.

Broadcasting Act (S.C. 1991, c. 11). Canada. Retrieved March 8, 2015 from http://canlii.ca/t/52d9x.

CBC inquiry concludes management mishandled Jian Ghomeshi. (2015, April 16). *CBC News.*Retrieved April 30, 2015, from http://www.cbc.ca/news/cbc-inquiry-concludes-management-mishandled-jian-ghomeshi-1.3035574.

Cormack, P., & Cosgrave, J. (2014). Theorising the state celebrity: A case study of the Canadian Broadcasting Corporation. *Celebrity Studies*, 321-339. Retrieved March 10, 2015, from http://www.tandfonline.com.libaccess.lib.mcmaster.ca/doi/abs/10.1080/19392397.2014.911111#.

Donovan, K., & Brown, J. (2014, October 26). CBC fires Jian Ghomeshi over sex allegations. *Toronto Star*. Retrieved October 30, 2014, from http://www.thestar.com/news/canada/2014/10/26/cbc_fires_jian_ghomeshi_over_sex_allegations.html.

Donovan, K., & Hasham, A. (2014, November 4). Former York University student alleges Ghomeshi fondled him. *Toronto Star*. Retrieved November 6, 2014, from http://www.thestar.com/news/canada/2014/11/04/ghomeshi_was_focus_of_complaints_during_york_student_days.html.

Full text: Jian Ghomeshi's Facebook post on why he believes CBC fired him. (2014, October 27). *Global News*. Retrieved March 8, 2015, from http://globalnews.ca/news/1637310/full-text-jian-ghomeshis-post-on-why-he-believes-cbc-fired-him/.

Ghomeshi, J. (2012). *1982*. Toronto: Viking.

Halberstam, J. (1995). *Skin shows: Gothic horror and the technology of monsters*. Durham: Duke University Press.

Heberle, R. (1996). Deconstructive Strategies and the Movement Against Sexual Violence. *Hypatia*, 63-76.

Keohane, K. (1997). *Symptoms of Canada: An essay on the Canadian identity*. Toronto: University of Toronto Press.

Kingston, A. (2014, November 6). Jian Ghomeshi: How he got away with it. *Maclean's*. Retrieved April 16, 2014, from http://www.macleans.ca/news/canada/jian-ghomeshi-how-he-got-away-with-it/.

Marshall, P. (2010). The promotion and presentation of the self: Celebrity as marker of presentational media. *Celebrity Studies,* 35-48. Retrieved July 15, 2015, from http://www.tandfonline.com.libaccess.lib.mcmaster.ca/doi/full/10.1080/19392390903519057#.

Marshall, W. (1996). The sexual offender: Monster, victim, or everyman? *Sexual Abuse: A Journal of Research and Treatment*, 8(4), 317-335. Retrieved August 9, 2015, from http://sax.sagepub.com.libaccess.lib.mcmaster.ca/content/8/4/317.full.pdf+html.

Mason, P., & Monckton-Smith, J. (2008). Conflation, collocation and confusion: British press coverage of the sexual murder of women. *Journalism*, 691-710. Retrieved September 12, 2015, from http://resolver.scholarsportal.info.libaccess.

lib.mcmaster.ca/resolve/14648849/v09i0006/691_ccac.xml.

Nandy, S. (2015). *Fame in Hollywood North: A Theoretical Guide to Celebrity Cultures in Canada.* Toronto: WaterHill Publishing.

O'Hara, S. (2012). Monsters, playboys, virgins and whores: Rape myths in the news media's coverage of sexual violence. *Language and Literature,* 247-259. Retrieved August 4, 2015, from http://resolver.scholarsportal.info.libaccess.lib.mcmaster.ca/resolve/09639470/v21i0003/247_mpvawrnmcosv.xml.

Puar, J. (2007). *Terrorist assemblages: Homonationalism in queer times.* Durham: Duke University Press.

Roth, M. (2014, October 19). Canada's 'Q' host Jian Ghomeshi speaks of life as an immigrant. *Pittsburgh Post-Gazette.* Retrieved April 15, 2015, from http://www.post-gazette.com/news/world/2014/10/19/Canada-s-Q-host-Jian-Ghomeshi-speaks-of-life-as-an-immigrant/stories/201410200001.

Rubinoff, J. (2014, October 31). Rubinoff: Jian Ghomeshi's shattered credibility. *The Waterloo Region Record.* Retrieved April 15, 2015, from http://www.therecord.com/whatson-story/4955411-rubinoff-jian-ghomeshi-s-shattered-credibility/.

Semple, J. (2014, November 7). In eyes of the world's media, Canada has lost its innocence: Jeff Semple. *CBC News.* Retrieved September 28, 2015, from http://www.cbc.ca/news/canada/in-eyes-of-the-world-s-media-canada-has-lost-its-innocence-jeff-semple-1.2826584.

Smart, C. (2002). *Feminism and the power of law.* London: Routledge.

Soothill, K., Walby, S., & Bagguley, P. (1990). Judges, the Media, and Rape. *Journal of Law and Society,* 211-233. Retrieved September 12, 2015, from http://www.jstor.org/stable/1410086.

Stermac, L. E., Du Mont, J. A., & Kalemba, V. (1995). Comparison of sexual assaults by strangers and known assailants in an urban population of women. *CMAJ: Canadian Medical Association Journal, 153*(8), 1089-1094. Retrieved September 10, 2015, from http://www.ncbi.nlm.nih.gov.libaccess.lib.mcmaster.ca/pmc/articles/PMC1487328/.

Walby, S., Hay, A., & Soothill, K. (1983). The Social Construction of Rape. *Theory, Culture & Society,* 86-98. Retrieved September 10, 2015, from http://resolver.scholarsportal.info.libaccess.lib.mcmaster.ca/resolve/02632764/v02i0001/86_tscor.xml.

Willms, J. (2015, January 8). Timeline of Jian Ghomeshi story. *Toronto Star.* Retrieved March 6, 2015, from http://www.thestar.com/news/gta/2015/01/08/timeline_of_jian_ghomeshi_story.html.

Wynne-Jones, L. (2014, November 6). "Ghomeshi-gate" Proves Why Every Man Should Be a Feminist. *Huffington Post Canada.* Retrieved April 15, 2014, from http://www.huffingtonpost.ca/lewis-wynnejones/jian-ghomeshi-feminism_b_6117330.html.

PART IV

Bridging Women's Issues and Media Representation

The Power of Celebrity Culture and its Response to Rape and Sexual Violence against Women in Post-2012 India

Nidhi Shrivastava

Abstract. December 2012 was a significant moment in Indian history when a young woman was raped heinously on a moving bus in Delhi. Her untimely death put India on the international media map and became the site of contemporary debates about women's rights in the country. As a result, many celebrities responded to the heinous crime and many documentaries and commercial films emerged as a response to the rape case in popular culture. Bollywood megastar Aamir Khan also featured an entire talk show episode on rape and sexual violence in India in his show, *Satyamev Jayate* (2012). Subsequent episodes also engaged in a discussion of eve-teasing. My chapter will specifically focus on the intersections between celebrity culture in India, post-colonial feminist theory, glamour and fame. How does the Delhi rape case reinforce or subvert celebrity culture? Popular actresses such as Deepika Padukone and Kalki Koelchin have been seminal in promoting women's rights and tackling sexism in India. I would like to explore the relationship between celebrities in India and how their response to significant issues of women's rights, feminism, and sexism were further complicated as a result of the Delhi rape case. What was the role Aamir Khan, Deepika Padukone, and Kalki Koelchin played to engage with the issue of rape and sexual violence?

Keywords: 2012 Delhi Rape Case, Aamir Khan, Deepika Padukone, Kalki Koelchin, Rape, Sexism, Post-colonial Feminist theory, women's rights, India

Introduction

The untimely heinous gang rape and death of Jyoti Singh Pandey, put India on the international map drawing national and international media attention to the glaring issues of violence against women in the country. Pandey became fondly known as 'Nirbhaya' ("fearless one"), 'Jagruti' ("awareness"), Damini ("lightening"), and Delhi braveheart and was the focus of numerous documentaries including the polemic Leslee Udwin's *India's Daughter* (2015) and British journalist Radha Bedi's *India: A Dangerous Place To Be A Woman* (2013). The response, however, was not only limited to journalists and documentary filmmakers but famous celebrities also became advocates for women's rights and sexism in India. In particular, my chapter will focus on Aamir Khan, who is not only an international celebrity and film actor but also is the host of a famous talk show, *Satyamev Jayate* (2012) that has covered vast number of social and political issues, which have been haunting India. In addition, Deepika Padukone and Kalki Koelchin have been seminal in promoting women's rights and tackling sexism in India. In this chapter, I explore the relationship between celebrities in India and how their response to significant issues of women's rights, feminism, and sexism was further complicated as a result of the Delhi rape case. What was the role that Aamir Khan, Deepika Padukone, and Kalki Koelchin played to engage with the issue of rape and sexual violence?

An In-Depth Analysis: The 2012 Delhi Rape Case

On December 16, 2012, Jyoti Singh Pandey was returning home with her male friend, Awindra Pratap Pandey when she was brutally beaten and raped by a group of joyriders. One of the four rapists who is currently serving a life sentence in Tihar Jail in Delhi, Mukesh Singh reportedly said in an interview with Leslee Udwin in *India's Daughter* (2015) that "a girl is far more responsible for rape than a boy ... A decent girl won't roam around at nine o'clock at night ... Housework and housekeeping is for girls, not roaming in discos and bars at night doing wrong things, wearing wrong clothes" (*The Guardian*). His controversial words sparked a nationwide controversy, which led to an eventual ban on the documentary. However, this rape case became a turning point in women's rights debate in India. Singh's comments also alluded to rape culture and its need to constantly blame the rape victim.

Class also played a key role in sensationalizing the Delhi rape case. Even though Jyoti Singh's family belonged to a lower class, both her parents were progressive believing in the education of their children. Belonging to a village where education was not considered valuable for boys or girls, Mr. Singh vowed to educate his children without any gender discrimination. He sold his agricultural land in his village and worked two shifts a day at the airport to pay for his daughter's education. In an interview with *India Ink* (2013), Singh recalled, "It never entered our hearts to ever discriminate, how could I be happy if my son is happy and my daughter isn't? And it was impossible to refuse a little girl who loved going to school." Therefore, the brutal gang rape illuminates the complexities and nuances in India's rape culture.

Furthermore, it is hard to overlook the role of Indian commercial cinema and equally important response of Bollywood celebrities after the horrific incident, which caused protests and national furor against the rapists. The Delhi rape case subverted Indian celebrity culture, because celebrities were forced to defend and promote the issue of violence against women in India. Rape culture condemns middle-and lower-class women and women from socially conservative regions who attempt to embrace a seemingly more modern lifestyle. Bollywood often portrays such lifestyles where women are empowered to make their own life decisions, become socially mobile, choose their own life partners, or dress or behave untraditionally. As such, Bollywood celebrities play a role in breaking down social conservatism vis-à-vis women's social roles. In particular, Aamir Khan, Deepika Padukone, and Kalki Koelchin have been vocal about women's rights, gender politics, and rape in India. Their role as advocates in this issue, specifically, highlights sexist social mores and celebrity campaign against it.

Item Numbers

Female celebrities are constantly under fire and arguably occupy a precarious position in the media. In other words, they not only play the roles of advocates for women's issues but also perform "item numbers" in numerous Indian films. Their characters in films are also less traditional, more sexually and socially independent. That being said, it is not hard to see that celebrities such as Padukone and Chopra have to justify their position as advocates in the media. The contemporary Indian cinema industry represents conflicting images of young Indian women. Rita Banerji (2014) in "Bollywood Baffled over Sex, Rape, and Prostitution" points out that Bollywood commercial actresses have started performing explicit "item" numbers, usually a cameo, with raunchier dance moves, lyrics, and scantily clad outfits. Popular actresses such as Deepika Padukone are usually depicted as sexually, socially, and economically independent women. Their representations suggest that this type of agency is available to women of all classes, especially since young women from all classes tend to view these actresses as role models. Their item numbers simultaneously objectify them sexually while also giving them an opportunity to express their sexuality. These heroines are usually portrayed as upper and middle class who have access to a cosmopolitan lifestyle, drink, attend nightclubs, are career oriented, and expressive of their needs and desires. The Indian film industry sells this fantasy to women from all classes and castes. Unfortunately, when caste enfranchised women from middle class participate or even desire to participate in these activities, they face misogynistic and patriarchal systems of oppression because women's access to the public sphere, threatens the hyper masculine public order. Mukesh Singh, for example, mentions that women's place is at home and as a result, women who defy this order are deserving of rape and violence. People also tend to conflate middle class lifestyle with western modes of living, and are resistant to it.

By participating in item numbers, these celebrities are vulnerable to criticism. An article in Bollywood tabloid *Pinkvilla* (2012) comments:

> When a celebrity openly condemns law and justice yet participates in the making and showcase of songs like these with some vulgar lyrics or

choreography does it not spell hypocrisy on their part? More importantly, these songs provide fodder for objectifying women, which is the issue that we are all trying to address. This is not just confined to films as an art form per se, but all others. But where do we draw the line between value and vulgarity? And films do not only have the responsibility to entertain, but also inform and reform. What is your stand on this issue? What is the real role of Bollywood celebrities in this case?

These criticisms further underline the sexism that is inherent within India's entertainment industry. It is important to note how celebrities make preemptive efforts to ward off such criticism. For instance, Deepika Padukone has been rumored to be in a relationship with her co-star Ranveer Singh. In an interview with *Economic Times* (2015), Padukone has said, "Something that happens in films is something I would not subscribe to in real life. I am traditional and conservative when it comes to relations." The words 'traditional' and 'conservative' indicate that she wants to make a distinction between the roles she plays as an actor and her true self outside of the silver screen.

Deepika Padukone – "It's My Choice"

Being the daughter of a celebrity sport star, Prakash Padukone who is close to Shah Rukh Khan, Padukone debuted in 2008 with Bollywood Badshaah (king), as Shah Rukh Khan is called, in *Om Shanti Om* (2007). She is the founder of the Live, Love, and Laugh Foundation. The foundation addresses depression, mental anxiety, and seeks to provide resources and acceptance for people who are coping with mental health issues.

Deepika Padukone has also been a proponent for women's rights issues. Released earlier in 2015, a recent advertisement in which she volunteered called "It's My Choice" has been criticized as "hypocritical." Directed by Homi Adjania who worked with her in other films, the video features popular women such as Anupama Chopra, actress Nimrat Kaur, and Farah Khan to bring awareness of women's rights in black-and-white frames, exposing their vulnerabilities but also demonstrating their strengths for being proud of their choices. In other words, Padukone as the narrator advocates that women have the choice to get married or not, to have control over their sexual desires, and for the choice to have ownership of their bodies. Unfortunately, while the message of the video is somewhat powerful, it should have arguably shown a mix of images documenting women from all classes and castes. Instead, it showed examples of women who already had class privilege to perhaps make choices, which lower class and caste women do not have. According to *Quartz India*:

> Vogue and Padukone have a lot in common: They're both from an industry that is based on fetishizing, objectifying and reinforcing sexist standards of beauty on women. So when these two forces combined talk about women's [sic] empowerment, one is left a bit confused, because, let's be honest, the [sic] fashion and Bollywood do not empower anyone—women most of all.

While the criticism is quite harsh, there is indeed some truth to it. While she narrates her rights to have a "choice," the video does not speak to their role in consumerist culture and also does not speak to the burden of choices which women have. Other critics such as Aseem Chabra have called the video "too urban, too upper class." Another critic from *Hindustan Times* posited, "Instead of talking about rape, female foeticide, domestic violence, harassment at workplace, pay gap, the intrusive male gaze or a million other issues that a woman has to deal with every day, the video chose to talk about topics which are plain bizarre." The video may not specifically articulate each of the aforementioned issues, it does suggest that women have a choice to live the way they choose to have an arranged marriage, have pre-marital sex, or have a career, which is indeed a powerful and influential message. What is interesting again is the contradictory remarks Padukone makes when questioned about the video itself? In an interview with *The Hindu* (2015) she says:

> When the script was shared with me, there was not one but a couple of lines that even I didn't agree with at a personal level but I realised they needed me more for the larger message the film was trying to make. I went ahead and was more than happy to be a part of it because I realised myself that there was a larger issue that we were dealing with and that we are dealing with. Just like the other 98 women who were the [sic] part of the video, I agreed to be a part of it.

Here, again we see that Padukone is defensive of *her* choices. Even though the advertisement's larger message was that women actually are entitled to make choices to shape their lives, Padukone is left in a predicament having to separate herself from a couple of lines she disagreed with on a "personal level." So far, it can be inferred that she is coping as both a celebrity female figure and a woman she is off-screen. Thus she is constantly in defense of her character, however, and even of her personal choices to create a video on female empowerment.

Kalki Koelchin – It's All My Fault

Ever since the rape of a Mumbai journalist in 2013, Kalki Koechlin and VJ Juhi Pande teamed up together with Indian comedy group called *All India Bakchod* (AIB). The video, *It's All My Fault*, went viral on YouTube but surprisingly was only mentioned briefly on my Facebook without any comments or reaching the same popularity that many other videos have received. Within a span of 3 minutes and 36-second footage, the video addresses popular topics like wearing provocative clothing, marital rape, late night parties, and going out for dates as means by which women bring rape and violence unto themselves As we live and breathe in the digital era, this does provoke concerns and thought because India continues to be viewed as a dangerous country for women. It also provokes questions about how we receive and process information and news. The video targets all the stereotypes and also engages with the law - where - it all boils down to victim blaming. Furthermore, it also pokes humor at many critics who said that the woman who was raped in December 2012 could have prevented the rape by shouting "bhaiya" (older brother in Hindi) and mocks statements made by politicians, *gurus*, and other people who blame that women trigger rape and bring it upon themselves.

Koechlin is an Indian actress of French descent, born to Joel Koelchin and Francoise Françoise Armandie, at the Sri Aurobindo Ashram in Auroville, Puducherry. Her parents are devotees of Sri Aurobindo. Koelchin studied drama and theatre at University of London. By being able to speak multiple languages, she made a debut in the Indian cinema *Dev D* (2009). Unlike Padukone, Koechlin's persona is based on her persona as an "outsider" in the Indian cinema. According to an interview, Koechlin told *India West*, "While the producers of 'Dev D' directly contacted me to audition for the role of Chanda, Anurag Kashyap was completely against the idea. After seeing my portfolio, Anurag rejected me stating that I am not an Indian and do not fit the role." Despite the initial rejection, she still reached her stardom after the release of the film. In the movie, she was cast as Chanda who was a victim of a MMS scandal, when her then-boyfriend released a porn video of her taped and released in the nation. Her family rejects her while her father ends his life due to embarrassment. I claim that Koechlin's casting as Chanda was deliberate and suggested that Indian women would never participate in pre-marital sex and therefore, it is impossible to imagine an actress like Deepika Padukone in a similar role. Surprisingly, Koechlin's perspectives on celebrity activism and feminism differ greatly from Padukone's. According to an interview with *Hindustan Times*, Koelchin (2014) observes:

I think it's a mix of many things. An actor can speak of these issues only if the media is conscious and chooses to highlight them. You are a part of the system you live in. Today a woman has a lot more status in public. Many more of her personality traits are being discussed, not just her beauty. So it is a good time to be heard. Having said that, I do believe it is the responsibility of everyone to be conscious and not just actors. An actor doesn't have to be an activist. Also, for actors it is important to associate themselves with issues that really matter to them, on which they can speak with authority, so that one doesn't end up looking like a poster girl for that cause. It's a double-edged sword. In the past only very hard-core activists for women's rights were referred to as feminists. The word had a negative undertone. Today it is fashionable for a woman, and even a man, to be termed a feminist, which is fantastic. At the same time, I feel, we have to think outside the label. As long as there is an imbalance in society it is most natural for those affected by it to speak about it and demand equality.

From her comments, Koechlin's advocacy as a celebrity activist differs greatly from the persona, which Padukone has created for herself in the Indian cinema. According to scholar Rajani Mazumdar who studies the figure of the westernized "vamp", the traditional heroines were always clad in traditional saris, sang songs, but remained sexually and culturally modest. The vamp figure, on the other hand, who seductively danced to 'cabaret' songs, emerged in Indian cinema in the 1950s, but continued to remain a common theme in the 1960s and 70s. The figure of the vamp was depicted as an "outsider" who had "distinct qualities from the woman of the nation (Mazumdar)." Mazumdar observes, "the vamp's body suggested excess, out of control desire, and vices induced by "Western" license. The vamp usually occupied public spaces of the casino/bar/nightclub, often as a floor show artist." This was especially true of films of the 1950s. Now, the tables have turned and Indian actresses such as Deepika Padukone compete to perform "item numbers." The item numbers were then viewed as short-cuts to successes for actresses because the consumerism of sexually explicit song and video not only promoted the film, but ensured their popularity. By participating in these "item numbers" such as the brief video of *Dum Maro Dum*, Padukone and Chopra are objectified in the screen for commercial gain. Therefore, Padukone's work as an outspoken feminist runs into trouble and complicates her persona as a celebrity advocate.

Aamir Khan – *Satyamev Jayate* (2012)

Aamir Khan belongs to an illustrious family, which has been part of the Hindi film industry. Born to Tahir Hussain, Khan made his debut in the late 1980s starring with Juhi Chawla in *Qyamat Se Qyamat Tak* (1988). In the 1980s and 90s, he played the chocolate boy starring in films such as *Hum Hai Rahi Pyaar Ke* (1989) and *Dil* (1990). Later, he achieved his stardom by starring in films such as *Lagaan* (2001), *Mangal Pandey: The Rising* (2005), *Rang De Basanti* (2006), *Fanaa* (2006), *Taare Zameen Par* (2006), *3 Idiots* (2009), and finally *Talaash* (2012) and *PK* (2014). These recent successes catapulted him to international stardom as his films dealt with prevalent social issues such as dyslexia, terrorism, women's rights, and the problems associated with the educational system and religious organizations in India.

Aamir Khan launched STAR India Network's *Satyamev Jayate* (*Truth Alone Prevails*) on May 2012. The series, which has now released about three seasons, focuses on glaring issues that are inherent in India's socio-economic fabric such as female foeticide, rape, masculinity and mental health. In 1988 B.R. Chopra's *The Mahabharata* aired on DD (Door Darshan) National on Sunday afternoons. At this time, the entire nation would be glued to the television screen embracing the political, social, and religious sentiments that created the classic Hindu epic. In 2012 *Satyamev Jayate*, aired on Sunday afternoons like *The Mahabharata*, arguably generated a similar impact on the Indian audiences. The event echoed nation-building when entire India, as with *The Mahabharata*, was united for a specific time watching the show that was emblematic of the nation's traditions and customs. The show also aired in various vernacular languages from India including Bengali, Malaylam, Tamil, and was also subtitled in English to ensure that the show reached maximum number of audiences. The first season of *Satyamev Jayate* also reached an international audience with audiences as far as North America and Sierra Leone. There was also special screening held in villages in Gujarat, Maharashtra, and Uttar Pradesh. According to leading Indian newspaper, *DNA*, this initiative was taken to ensure that the issues of the "common man" reached the populations who had limited television connectivity. The first show that was aired focused on female foeticide and its implications. Unfortunately, there is limited scholarship on the stardom of Aamir Khan and in particular, his relationship as a host to the show. Akshaya Kumar, a doctoral candidate from University of Glasgow, contends that Khan uses sacrifice as a trope in order to reinforce his political agency. By becoming a sacrificial figure, he reinforces his moral authority and addresses the grievances and issues that are currently plaguing India. Kumar (2014) also adds:

> The sacrificial ritual enunciated by Khan, on the other hand, demands that the star be reborn, not re-produced. He must retain a consistency with his essence and performance, yet perform the new. Such a sacrifice is impossible without a gap or an absence to mark the end of one cycle

and the beginning of another. This is ultimately unproductive for the creation of global capital. Therefore, resistance to the economic surplus must mark the re-birth in sacrificial mode... We must see Khan's decision to not appear in advertisements at the beginning of *Satyamev Jayate* as boundary-work: marking the constitutive outside of his show, indicating his departure from his film-stardom cycle. (p. 245)

Kumar addresses a significant turning point in Khan's career. The departure from the "film-stardom cycle" is apparent in the episodes of *Satyamev Jayate*, in particular the show on rape that was a direct response to the 2012 Delhi Rape Case. In this particular episode, Khan argued that the medical, legislative, law, and societal fronts should address the rights of women, especially of the rape victim. In particular, women should not be victimized and humiliated further if they have already experienced trauma. The society points the finger at the raped woman rather than blame the rapist for his heinous crime.

According to an interview with Iraqi-American Humanitarian Zainab Salbi, founder of Women for Women organization, Khan (2015) comments that "the balance of power in India needs to change. Unless conviction becomes swift and certain, things are not going to change in India. And very importantly, as a society we have to shun the rapist and hold the survivor close." Furthermore, he observes that masculinity in India needs to be re-defined. He argues, "Is a real man someone who goes and beats up people, is a real man a person who is the protector... Unless we re-look at and hopefully re-define what a man is, things are not going to change." Aamir Khan's dedication to social issues reinforces the celebrity culture especially in regards to the Delhi rape case. For example, his privilege as a male and therefore, access to certain gendered and class privileges is left unquestioned when he is on stage of *Satyamev Jayate*. He is indeed seen as having a "self-sacrificing" persona because he is gravely concerned for the well-being of Indian society and less so, for his own material privileges. Although he does not identify himself as an activist, his celebrity stardom inadvertently defines his persona as a concerned citizen-subject. His persona is comparable with Tom Hanks – a man who is concerned and immersed in societal issues, which are larger than his stardom.

Conclusion

Aamir Khan, Kalki Koechlin, and Deepika Padukone hold variant degrees of star power especially when it comes to advocacy for women's rights. These actors represent the complexities and nuances of the gendered politics, which are inherent within India's popular culture. Aamir Khan's *Satyamev Jayate* actually makes him more relatable than Koechlin and Padukone because he portrays himself on-screen as a "sacrificial" figure and a "common" man who cares about the prevalent issues, which are currently plaguing India's social fabric. Koechlin and Padukone, on the other hand, are viewed as powerful advocates for women's rights. While Koechlin seems to come across as more intellectual of the two, Padukone's celebrity status leaves her in a problematic position. On one hand, she promotes women's rights, but on the other hand, she herself is part of the system that ensures women are viewed as sexual objects by male (and female) consumers especially when she performs as an "item" girl.

References

Aamir Khan: Masculinity in India must be redefined to combat rape, violence against women. (2015, April 23). *The Financial Express*. Retrieved from http://www.financialexpress.com/article/lifestyle/showbiz/aamir-khan-masculinity-in-india-must-be-redefined-to-combat-rape-violence-against-women/66195/

Anurag Initially Rejected Me for 'Dev D': Kalki Koechlin. (2014, July 18). *India West*. Retrieved from http://www.indiawest.com/entertainment/bollywood/anurag-initially-rejected-me-for-dev-d-kalki-koechlin/article_e8f7cd7c-0ebd-11e4-8e89-001a4bcf887a.html

Banerjee, P. An actor doesn't have to be an activist: Kalki Koechlin. (2016, January 13). *The Hindustan Times*. Retrieved from http://www.hindustantimes.com/bollywood/an-actor-doesn-t-have-to-be-an-activist-kalki-koechlin/story-AXPYKF45jlaYCXNXJtjtcP.html

Banerji, R. (2013). Bollywood baffled over sex, rape and prostitution. Gender Forum, (46), 1. Retrieved from http://search.proquest.com/docview/1501552273?accountid=15115

Bawa, J. S. (2015, April 1). Sorry Deepika Padukone, these are not the choices women need. *The Hindustan Times*. Retrieved from http://www.hindustantimes.com/bollywood/sorry-deepika-padukone-these-are-not-the-choices-women-need/story-sjkcRzCx8j48InY9VcP28N.html

Delhi Gang-Rape Case: Do Celebs have a responsibility? (2012, December 21). *Pinkvilla*. Retrieved fromhttp://www.pinkvilla.com/entertainmenttags/celebrities/delhi-gang-rape-case-do-celebs-have-responsibility

I didn't endorse infidelity in 'My Choice': Deepika Padukone. (2015, May 5). *The Hindu*. Retrieved from http://www.thehindu.com/entertainment/i-didnt-endorse-infidelity-in-my-choice-deepika-padukone/article7173531.ece

I'm conservative & traditional when it comes to relationships: Deepika Padukone (2015, December 20). *The Economic Times*. Retrieved from http://economictimes.indiatimes.com/magazines/panache/im-conservative-traditional-when-it-comes-to-relationships-deepika-padukone/articleshow/50255506.cms

Kumar, A. (2014). Satyamev Jayate: Return of the Star as a Sacrificial Figure. *South Asia: Journal of South Asian Studies* Vol. 37 (2), 239-254. Doi: 10.1080/00856401.2014.906087

Mazumdar, R. (c2007). *Bombay Cinema: An Archive Of The City*. Minneapolis: University of Minnesota Press.

Rehman, M. (2015, March 4). India bans TV stations from showing interview with man who raped student. *The Guardian*. Retrieved from http://www.theguardian.com/world/2015/mar/03/india-outraged-interview-man-convicted-gang-rape-student

Sharma, B. (2013, December 16). A Year Later, Family of Delhi Gang Rape Victim Press for 'Full Justice.' *The New York Times*. Retrieved from http://india.blogs.nytimes.com/2013/12/16/a-year-later-family-of-delhi-gang-rape-victim-press-forfulljustice/?_php=true&_type=blogs&_php=true&_type=blogs&_r=3

Special screening of 'Satyamev Jayate' in villages (2012, May 6). *DNA*. Retrieved from http://www.dnaindia.com/entertainment/report-special-screening-of-satyamev-jayate-in-villages-1685288

Sra, G. Deepika Padukone's video for Vogue is not empowering—it's hypocritical. (2015, March 30) .*Quartz India*. Retreived from http://qz.com/372373/deepika-padukones-video-for-vogue-is-not-empowering-its-hypocritical/

Media Representations and Angelina Jolie's Elective Mastectomy and Transnational Adoption

Basuli Deb

Abstract. Angelina Jolie's coming out after her double elective mastectomy to preempt breast cancer because of her high-risk genetics modeled for women unconventional preventive measures for cancer, and the media representation of it opened up new spaces for dialogue about women's health. Similarly, her transnational adoption and the media publicity around it that she consciously uses to propagate transnational adoptions from the global South has inspired more Americans to adopt from such countries. At the same time, this has given rise to intense criticism about a brand of celebrity colonialism that defines the relationship between the haves and have-nots across both the domestic and the international division of labor. However, in this era of globalized networks dominant forces are bound up with the disenfranchised in ways that demand thinking beyond pure oppositions. This paper will uncover the possibilities of negotiating difficult terrains of cross-class socially transformative work in women's rights when celebrities mingle with the public in common causes. In the process, it aims to shift elitist understandings of public intellectualism, with its ivory tower academic heritage, by foregrounding non-normative public intellectuals through Jolie's controversial humanitarian work. It interrogates the role of the media in bridging gaps between celebrity lifestyles and journalism to redefine how "gossip" itself can become a tool of social advocacy rather than a tool for denigrating celebrity talent.

Keywords: Transnational feminism, Angelina Jolie, left media and tabloids, breast cancer, adoption, celebrity activism, fandom

Introduction

Feminist studies with its zeal for social justice and its egalitarian aspiration has often viewed celebrities with suspicion for their tremendous social power. This is intensified in the case of celluloid celebrities because of their financial power. Few feminist critics have examined how the social power of celluloid celebrities and their inextricable link to capital can be harnessed for social transformation. However, the field of feminist studies has taken a critical turn with the interjection of transnational feminism and its critical insurgencies. Transnational feminism has critiqued the us versus them binary logic of imperialist feminism obsessed with "saving" the *other* – the women of the elsewhere – in the same breath as it has critiqued postcolonial feminism for its refusal to engage with the territory of the *self*-identities that cannot be deemed as disempowered despite being marked by gender differentials. With its unbound energies that cross borders and boundaries transnational feminism then becomes key in uncovering the possibilities of celebrity negotiations of difficult terrains of cross-class engagement when celluloid celebrities such as Angelina Jolie find themselves inextricably bound with those of others who find themselves on the other side of the power divide. In the process of examining personal decisions of celebrities that intersect with humanitarian work for those others, this chapter aims to shift elitist understandings of public intellectualism with its long-standing associations with scholars and writers by foregrounding non-normative public intellectuals like Jolie.

Angela Jolie: The Brand Identity

Angelina Jolie is a brand identity, and her brand is not merely defined by the Hollywood logo, but by the diversification of her career into a public figure as she seamlessly intertwines her Hollywood image as one of the sexiest and most beautiful women in the world with that of one of the most influential people in the world, derived both from her celebrity status and her social advocacy work. Daughter of award winning Hollywood star Jon Vogt, Jolie's Hollywood career has been decorated with numerous awards and her superstardom has brought immense publicity to her award winning humanitarian work for refugees, women's rights, environmental justice, and education. In fact, Jolie's is a story of rebranding (Clark, 2012). From an actor with a dysfunctional relationship with her father and unstable romantic relationships, prone to mental health breakdown that included eating disorder and self-injury culminating in suicidal attempts, who openly shared details about her sex life with the media and gained notoriety, Jolie became the beloved of the media. She came to be represented as a devoted and gentle mother of a large family combining biological and transnationally adopted children, and a thoughtful humanitarian honored as the Goodwill Ambassador of the United Nations High Commissioner for Refugees at their Geneva headquarters. In fact, her transnational motherhood came to be inextricably tied to her humanitarian work as well as her films when she adopted her first transnational child from Cambodia in 2002 after she filmed there for a Lara Croft movie and found herself involved with refugee issues. In 2013, against the tide of feminist disengagement with mainstream celluloid celebrities of the likes of Jolie as transformational figures, a feminist solidarity politics ensued as the Jolie made public to the media her cancer preventive double mastectomy. Thus, Angelina Jolie's rebranding becomes an increasingly important site of feminist critical analysis as she enters the domain of serious intellectual work through her radical rethinking of health and motherhood. Such work in turn creates shifts in public understandings of such issues as well as domains of expert knowledge that influence action on the ground, generating feminist *praxis* (intersection of theory and practice). A personal anecdote here will describe my first attempt at an intervention into this debate about the possibilities and impossibilities of social transformation work by celebrities such as Jolie.

Breast Cancer

In the May 25, 2013 issue of *Dissident Voices: A Radical Newsletter in the Struggle for Peace and Social Justice*, Deepa Kumar published a signature petition called "Leftist Sexism" to disagree with Ruth Fowler's columns in *Counterpunch* that had criticized Angelina Jolie's *New York Times* essay about her decision to have double mastectomy to preempt breast cancer because of her high-risk genetics (Kumar, 2013). In a move of transnational feminist solidarity, I signed the petition along with other feminist scholars and activists from USA, Canada, the UK, Netherlands, and India. In her essay Jolie clearly states her motives in publicizing her decision lies in her "hope that other women can benefit from my experience" (Jolie, 2013). She adds: "I choose not to keep my story private because there are many women who do not know that they might be living under the shadow of cancer." She recognizes the impact that such a disclosure about cancer preventive decision making from a celebrity of her status will have on the preemptive healthcare choices of her female fans: "For any woman reading this, I hope it helps you to know you have options. I want to encourage every woman, especially if you have a family history of breast or ovarian cancer, to seek out the information and medical experts who can help you through this aspect of your life, and to make your own informed choices." She also invokes her huge male fandom enthralled by her celebrity appeal as she includes them in her social advocacy message about women's elective healthcare. She addresses their role as supportive partners in this demanding as well as life restorative process, foregrounding her own partner Brad Pitt's role in her preemptive double elective mastectomy: "I am fortunate to have a partner, Brad Pitt, who is so loving and supportive. So to anyone who has a wife or girlfriend going through this, know that you are a very important part of the transition." Fowler had undermined Jolie's credibility to speak for survivors of breast cancer because of the economic means unavailable to other women that Jolie had for such an expensive medical procedure (Fowler, 2013), and because the corporation Myriad Genetics was generating huge profits from screening tests for breast cancer.

In other words, Fowler's critique of Jolie's *New York Times* article is situated in a left-wing critique of the "medical-industrial complex, including its government lackeys, who sustain the class disparities of the for-profit health care system" (Smith, 2013). It is grounded in a critique of celebrity colonialism where the social power of celebrities is seen as threatening to the well-being of society because of its potentiality to appropriate the less privileged while remaining divorced from the socioeconomic realities of their material lives. Within such a framework of celebrity colonialism, what Jolie is advocating becomes a proprietory act as the celebrity colonial gaze claims to know that astronomically expensive healthcare only celebrities can afford will be best for all women irrespective of their class locations. However, in this context Sharon Smith has pointed out to the implications of the subtitle "Of Privilege, Health Care and Tits" that the editors added to Fowler's article, and the ridicule in Fowler's allusion to Jolie's "elaborately reconstructed chest." Underlining the failure of the left to engage in a sound gender politics, Smith argues: "But using boob jokes to introduce an article about undergoing a double mastectomy to prevent a potentially deadly disease constitutes a descent from sexism to misogyny." Deepa Kumar's petition that I referred to earlier similarly argued against Fowler's position that dehumanized Jolie's publicity about her mastectomy for social advocacy:

> When a "celebrity" such as Jolie speaks about double mastectomy not affecting her femininity she is bringing relief to many women who are caught in this trap of gender and class. And because she is a celebrity (who need not have exposed herself to such scrutiny we might add), she created a larger space in the mainstream media to reflect on these issues.

Deepa Kumar who is an Associate Professor of Media Studies and Middle East Studies at Rutgers University was in the news last year for her anti-imperialist tweets about the War on Terror. She serves as my entry point into Jolie's controversial humanitarian work in the realm of transnational adoption. Why would an anti-imperialist scholar-activist like Kumar contest Fowler's critique of Jolie's class privilege and the corporatization of women's health? Why would so many transnational feminist scholar-activists sign such a petition? The answer lies not only in the petition's ethos to contest the sexism in Fowler's essays, but also in our appreciation of how Jolie opened up new spaces for dialogue about women's health. In other words, the very different reactions represented by the media and leftist thinkers who regularly write for such media foreground how even the media of the left that defines itself through its egalitarian social impulses somehow fall appallingly short of being inclusive when it comes to feminist visions of social justice. Moreover, in the face of a critique of celebrity colonialism, if one were to ask why something as personal and serious as Jolie's mastectomy became a selling point for various media outlets, one would arrive at an understanding of how celebrity lives are colonized as the media appropriates them through constant voyeuristic surveillance and reporting of their most intimate moments and decisions because celebrities such as Jolie, despite being talented artists and activists, remain commodified by the media because of their ability to generate capital.

Transnational Adoption

Despite their commodification, celebrities like Jolie also control information and representation as they maneuver their media interlocutors to influence their fandom for achieving political goals. Jolie's transnational adoption of three children—Maddox from Cambodia, Zahra from Ethiopia, and Pax from Vietnam and the media publicity around it that she consciously uses to propagate transnational adoptions from the global South has inspired more Americans to adopt from such countries. At the same time, this has given rise to intense criticism about a brand of celebrity colonialism that defines the relationship between the haves and have-nots across both the domestic and the international division of labor as celebrity lifestyles sway entire fandoms at home and abroad because fans emulate the lives of their stars and replicate their actions. Celebrity colonialism has often become the butt of social satire. In fact, in 2009 *Saturday Night Live* portrayed a skit of Angelina Jolie and Madonna fighting over who could outrun the other in adopting "spicy brown babies" from the "craziest" places in the world and in getting media attention for it. Like Jolie who adopted three children from countries in the global south, Madonna adopted David and Mercy from Malawi amidst much controversy. Erasing the private narratives of desire for family and kinship that superstars share with others, the skit offers the audience a parody of family formation across racial divides and caricatures women's non-biological expressions of transnational motherhood as shallow manifestations of imperialist desires and celebrity navel gazing. However, Robert Clarke (2009) argues, "the interpretation of contemporary postcolonial celebrity as either anachronistic or a vanguard of resurgent forms of cultural colonialism, may not adequately account for the power that such figures command across different audiences and communities" (p. 6). If so, it is here that celebrity power over society comes into conversation with the possibilities of harnessing that social command for the purposes of social transformation. This is a conversation about celebrities as public intellectuals. Whether such non-normative public intellectualism will be validated for its tremendous potentiality for social change or invalidated as celebrity quirks will depend on if tabloid journalism will use "gossip" about celebrity lifestyles as a tool for social advocacy rather than a tool for denigrating celebrity potential.

It is useful then to return to tabloid representations of Angelina Jolie's transnational adoption from the global south. The tabloids are now rife with the possibility of her and her partner Brad Pitt's adoption of the two-year old Syrian refugee boy Moussa whom Jolie as UN ambassador for refugees met at a refugee camp in Turkey in early 2015. Similarly in 2007, the tabloids were rife with the possibility of her adopting a child from the African nation of Chad in response to her adoption of two Asian children from Cambodia and Vietnam and another from Ethiopia. Vicious in its articulation, the tabloids render Jolie's transnational adoption into a racially charged and crude newspiece about political correctness:

> 'Angelina and Brad want to make sure Zahara doesn't feel alienated as the only black face in their family,' a source told London's News of the World. Jolie herself recently said, 'Should you balance the races, so there's another African person in the house for Zahara, after another Asian person in the house for Mad? We think so.' (Gossip.net 2007)

Incredibly crude in its targeting of Jolie's and Pitt's diverse and transnational family, the racist humor here turns Jolie's principled mothering and its intimate relationship to her humanitarian work for refugees into a representation of the white savior complex, demonstrating not only tabloids' uncomplicated understanding of celebrity colonialism, but also its own racist agendas. The backlash against Jolie for her attempt at privacy during the adoptions is intense. The headline on *Us Weekly* blasted her with: "Her Twisted Double Life," along with, "Her broken promise to be a stay-at-home mom . . . How she uses her kids to manipulate the media." *Star* lashed out: "Angelina Walks Out on Brad! . . . and Dumps the Kids!" (Gossip.net 2007). The media's fraught relationship with celebrity women discussed earlier in the context of the intellectual left's media controversies around misogynistic representations of Jolie's elective mastectomy is now reiterated in tabloid's virulent sexist portrayals of Jolie as the celebrity working woman – as the erratic, warped, and manipulative bad mother and wife. In such a representation Jolie's story is not only the story of celebrity colonialism of the transnational *other* of the white racial imaginary of imperialism, but also the story of the colonialization by empowered celebrity women of the *others* of the micropolitics of the family—the children and the husband. Ironically here, the media's colonization of celebrity women through a toxic rhetoric of patriarchal judgment then goes unquestioned as the sympathy of readers, themselves situated in the logic of a hetero-patriarchal society, is stirred up for the betrayed children and partner. With this crass misrepresentation of transnational adoption, what is erased is the personhood of the celebrity. The private desires of the celebrity parent that fans could have somewhat identified with are rendered distant as value judgments define the superstar as far removed from the morality of an ethical society where the woman is the signifier of stability and simplicity that keep the home intact for the husband and the children. What is lost in the process is the potentiality for social transformation when the private desires of celebrities bleed into the realm of public governance — when the mother in Jolie bleeds into the ambassador for the United Nations High Commissioner for Refugees.

Responsible Journalism

So, then what would responsible journalism look like? How would media negotiate between fandom, which thrives on celebrity gossip, and its responsibility to uphold ethical reporting? Can celebrity gossip have strategic usage for social transformation? If so, how do we productively harness gossip? I would argue that to reorient the values of a fandom, responsible journalism could use tabloid gossip around the lives of celebrity activists such as Jolie whose humanitarian work is seamlessly intertwined with their private lives. Instead of a gossip phenomenon that sets in opposition the mother/wife and the humanitarian, such gossip would portray how the mother feeds into the humanitarian. For instance, it would write stories about how Jolie is training her biological child Shiloh as a future humanitarian by taking her to zones of refugee crisis. The idea is to deploy the social phenomenon of gossip in meaningful ways to reconstruct the celebrity as a public intellectual. It is not a new role for the media. When the photograph of celebrity academic Edward Said throwing a stone in protest against the Israeli occupation of Palestine came under severe criticism, such a critique was deconstructed by academics and the media to foreground Said, with his distinguished academic heritage, as the quintessential public intellectual in solidarity with the dispossessed of Palestine. On the other hand, tabloids construct Jolie's stardom differently despite her contribution to humanitarian work, foregrounding the impossibility of a meaningful cross-class politics by claiming that any such engagement is merely a shallow manifestation of Jolie's fancy for the have-nots of the world. Responsible journalism could instead highlight the commonality between superstars such as Jolie and her fans, emphasizing ways in which her fans can relate to her as an ethical and responsible person, but also aware of her ability to activate social change in a way that is difficult for most of them. For instance, the media has been recently rife with gossip about Shiloh's transgender identity, and the supportive parenting that Jolie and Pitt have been providing Shiloh through a gender identity formation process. This offers powerful role models to fans who across class and geographical borders are faced with parenting children with non-normative gender and sexual identities. Responsible journalism can make a strategic move to harness the capital involved in celebrity gossip media to shift perspectives of fandom for social transformation work.

What purpose can this then serve on the ground to engage the fandom that celebrity gossip holds together? Perspectival shifts in the fandom can lead to a common-front politics of social transformation on the ground where celebrities and their fan base work together as forces of social change. I imagine a politics where celluloid celebrities like Jolie are reconstructed as public intellectuals, their talents nurtured by the media for the sustenance of their activism. The goal is to bring out the utilitarian potential of celebrity gossip to synergize the humanitarian energies of fans and their celebrity idols for action driven political tasks. Material effects of such a vision include celebrity-fan organizations for grassroots work, and venues for celebrities to articulate their social justice work in large public gatherings to disseminate and intensify as well as sustain such work. I also imagine venues for fans to come together to publicize their humanitarian work with their idols. With this strategic usage of fandom, newly launched humanitarian projects will immediately gather momentum as well as workers who can push social action forward. For instance, if we were to imagine a fan base for Angelina Jolie which was invested in transnational adoption in the context of refugee crisis that she works for, what kind of productive interventions would that have on US foreign policy toward efforts to mitigate refugee crises that more often than not result from imperial warfare and its trenchant legacies? How would transnational adoption by celebrities be situated differently when the reception of such work by the fandom is mediated not only by the tabloids, but also by the humanitarian work of fans alongside celebrities? The macropolitics of public governance and the micropolitics of the familial would then receive new understandings through media representations of celebrity humanitarian work and the fandom's engagement with such projects of social transformations, simultaneously as its relationship with its icon is redefined through fresh understandings of global citizenship.

A transnational feminist perspective on Jolie's transnational adoption then opens new avenues for understanding public intellectualism, and harnessing star power for social change through negotiations of difficult terrains of culture work. The key here is the struggle for ethical and responsible journalism to preserve celebrity talent for social justice activism by generating celebrity public intellectualism that bridge gaps with a fan base that activates social action rather than tabloids that cash in on the gaps between stars and their fans. The material goal is to establish a critical mass of organizations where celebrities and their fans come together for social justice action projects.

References

Celebrity—Gossip.net. (2007, April 5). Jolie and Pitt: Chad Adoption, Tabloid Enemies. *Gossipcenter.* Retrieved 20 January 2016, from http://es.celebrity-gossip.net/angelina-jolie?page=82

Clark, D. (2012, January 20). Branding lessons from Angelina Jolie. *Forbes*. Retrieved January 20, 2016, from http://www.forbes.com/sites/dorieclark/2012/01/20/branding-lessons-from-angelina-jolie/#50191e4a3295

Clark, R. (2009). The idea of celebrity colonialism: An introduction. In Robert Clark (Ed.), *Celebrity Colonialism: Fame, Power, and Representation in Colonial and Postcolonial Cultures* (pp. 1-12). Newcastle upon Tyne: Cambridge Scholars Press.

Fowler, R. (2013, May 14). Angelina Jolie under the knife. *Counterpunch*. Retrieved January 20, 2016, from http://www.counterpunch.org/2013/05/14/angelina-jolie-under-the-knife/

Jolie, A. (2013, May 13). My medical choice. *New York Times*. Retrieved January 20, 2016, from http://www.nytimes.com/2013/05/14/opinion/my-medical-choice.html?_r=0

Kumar, D. (2013, May 25). Leftist sexism. *Dissident Voices and Representative Authors*. Retrieved August 17, 2015, from http://dissidentvoice.org/2013/05/leftist-sexism/

Madonna and Angelina Jolie. *SNL*. Retrieved May 1, 2009, from http://www.nbc.com/Saturday_Night_Live/video/clips/updatemadonna-and-angelina-jolie/1081317

Smith, S. (2013, May 16). Why CounterPunch owes women an apology. *SocialistWorker.org*. Retrieved January 20, 2016, from http://socialistworker.org/2013/05/16/they-owe-women-an-apology

Made in the USA
Middletown, DE
02 May 2019